BETWEEN
IRAQ
AND A
HARD PLACE

My Year With Saddam Hussein

JOHN NORMAN

PAGE PUBLISHING, INC.
New York, NY

First originally published by Page Publishing, Inc. 2018

ISBN 978-1-64350-374-5 (Paperback)
ISBN 978-1-64350-375-2 (Digital)

Printed in the United States of America

In dedication to my late father,

John K. Norman

CHAPTER 1

Blowout in Bogotá

"Get me the fuck out of here!" I screamed into the telephone receiver.

"I can't explain it now, but everything went terribly wrong." Cathy Wilcox, our corporate travel agent in Washington, D.C., was usually great in these high-stress, no-time situations. Tonight was just not one of them.

"It's 8:30 p.m. your time, there is no one flying anywhere until the morning," she said. "Can't you get out on a private plane in any direction?"

"We don't have the dollars and I would not even know how to do it," I replied.

"There is a 7:30 a.m. on Avianca tomorrow. You're confirmed on it. Be there two hours early."

"Thanks, Cathy," I said. It was going to be a long night; one of the longest in my life!

I came to Columbia a few weeks earlier to participate in a routine review of electronic banking solutions for Banco de Occidente in Bogotá. We already had a team there for some nine months conducting a rather mundane operations review. Our offices, as well as our living accommodations, were in La Tecandama, a residence hotel of mediocre quality in downtown section of the city. Much later when cocaine king Pablo Escobar's family was camped out there, he blew the place up! Warm of him, wasn't it?

I knew something was wrong when the night representatives of the bank picked us up at the airport. They made us lie down on the floor of the jeep because we were out past curfew. They dropped us off in haste in the front of our hotel.

The gentleman who ran this project and the credit card division for the bank was Jorge Antonio Hector Morales. He had a beautiful flat in the city and a daughter who would give you a stiff one in a minute. Cartel paid? Quite possibly. He was teaching management at the university. Cartel arranged? Maybe. He was writing a book on management (I heard it stunk). He was also head of Information Technology for the bank (dumb idea). Jorge had the most annoying habit of getting right in front of your face, providing you with some discourse, turning on one heel, and flipping his tie over his shoulder with a snap. We all used to imitate him. The bank had a twenty-year relationship with IBM and I was out to break it. What I didn't know was how much cash was circulating as bribe money, and the bank was controlled by the Medellín cartel.

Jorge and I did not get along and I get along with everybody. This became painfully clear when he discovered I knew what I was doing and he did not. We took Jorge, his "assistant" Clara, and the finance director on a technology shopping trip to Florida. We showed them everything except what they came to see. It was a disaster. We stiffed them with a $700 dinner bill at an Orlando restaurant. Clara fawned over Jorge to a point that she even cut his meat for him so he could continue talking. I think when he went to take a leak she even dried off the head of his dick for him.

One member of our team was Wallace Jamison, a friend of my boss. He was allegedly an operations guru, but I think my boss was just paying off an old debt. Wallace, or "Uncle Wally," as our pubescent staff affectionately knew him, needed money to pay his daughter's college tuition loan. He had already been taken to the cleaners by a multitude of ex-wives. He was congenial and harmless, or so I thought.

Although I had long since given up spirits, one evening I sauntered down to the hotel bar just to see what I could see. The only patron at the bar was Uncle Wally. He was already blotto on whiskey. We carried on an incoherent conversation for a period of time until I got bored and wanted to leave. Uncle Wally was obviously dismayed that I did not drink.

"Do you know what a pisshead is?" he spluttered out.

Being quite familiar with the term from my youth in England, I replied that I did.

"Well, I'm a pisshead you see," he said with some degree of pride. You could have fooled me for the term refers to one who is rather drunk more frequently than usual for any occasion, like the sun coming up. I had met many of them. For the most part, they were sad cases with whom most for some reason took great pity on and always seemed to find a way to keep going, to stay employed. They usually possessed outlandish personalities.

Bogotá was a teeming shitpile of five million people; most of them living in abject poverty. The only "service" not subject to graft and corruption was the cartel themselves, for they were out in the open. Everyone else, even the President and judges, were payable. The Columbian military was all over the place but did little. There's nothing like the sight of a seventeen-year-old in full combat gear, sweating nervously from the forehead, trigger finger itching on an AK-47. Comforting, isn't it? You cannot go out with jewelry. Even during the day, thieves will run past you and grab it from your neck. Bodies hang from trees. Bombs explode in the wee hours of the morning. La Tecandama was the only hotel in the world I've stayed in that ran out of cold water. One lunch hour, a couple of men in a pickup truck with a tarp over the back drove to the central jail in the main plaza in downtown Bogotá. The place was packed with people eating a pita bread-type sandwich with "Manwich" in it. These guys whipped off the tarp and on the back was a small cannon. They fired at the wall of the jail putting a huge hole in it, scattering people in all directions amid the smoke and rubble, pulled their man out, blasted a few Federales into "Manwich" refills, kicked the cannon off the back and sped off. Nobody was in hot pursuit. In Columbia, you can come out of a business meeting with someone's arm around your neck embracing you, all smiles and radiant, and there would be a guy waiting around the corner of the building ready to slit your throat. Ah, South America!

Uncle Wally wanted to take me out on the town one evening. I was very reluctant to go. I already knew where we were going to wind up after Wally had been adequately fueled and we'd been thrown out of several tawdry bars. We stumbled into one of Wally's favorite bordellos. He was obviously well-known and well-liked, for the whores flocked around him like stink on shit. While he made a vain attempt to fend them off, smiling broadly, I had a seat on velvet, well-worn couch. Wally was organizing more alcohol, spreading around money here and there. He came over to me and said, "Go ahead, boy, I've set you up with the pick of the litter, two if you'd like."

I briefly considered running but had no idea in the middle of the barrio how to get out. The streets were beyond dangerous. I made a calculated risk of possibly what disease I could contract in pre-AIDS Columbia. The odds weren't too bad. I had a reasonable shot with soap, water, and penicillin. A young dark-skinned girl with deep-brown eyes approached me. She seemed to be the only one who had to guts to.

"I am Maria," she said coyly. "You like me?"

"Yes," I replied. "You're very lovely."

Uncle Wally stood off in the corner, beaming like a proud father, while fondling the tits of one girl and groping the other's ass with a spare hand. In Columbia, every girl's name was Maria, with six other names attached to it.

"*La coca?*" she inquired.

My past got the best of me. I figured just a line or two, and I'll force Uncle Wally out of the place with some subtle threat. Nothing doing there. This kid was no amateur. She took an atomizer from around her neck and stuffed it up one of my nostrils. I took a hard blast. Next, she fired up the other nostril, wiped my mustache, and handed me a glass of cold water. Wally already warned her I was the "Major Domo" and did not drink and not to fuck with me. I began to bleed from the nose. She gently tilted my head back. I could not feel my legs. I could not feel anything, but the blood coursing through my arteries, and my pants bulging. She moved her red lips closer. I could feel her breath on my face. She knew she had me, and so did everyone else in the room who gazed at me like I was some amusement, which I probably was. The bleeding subsided. The high remained.

"How old are you?" I asked.

"Twenty," she replied.

At this point, I couldn't be sure of anything. Before I regained some sense of composure, we were in a room upstairs. Maria undressed us both. She was beautiful, but well-traveled for her age. I could tell from the cigarette burns and small blade scars over various parts of her body. Rough players and bad deals; the street price of inexperience. She walked over with coke on her tongue and some in her hand, which she stuffed, into the head of my dick. She thrust her tongue down my throat and pushed me onto the bed. As the saying goes, "When in Rome, do as the Romans do!" She took me for the ride of my life for hours. The acts she performed were unfathomable to the once-a-month puritanism of Americans. Sometime later, I asked her again how old she was.

"Twenty," she again repeated.

"You're lying. You know it. How old are you?" I again pushed her.

"Okay, okay, I tell you. Eighteen!" she shouted.

She now began to kiss me and grab me again as I tried to shove her away.

"All right, Maria, we'll play a little game." She for the first time that night looked frightened. I took a hundred dollar bill and held it between two fingers in front of her face.

"One more time, how old are you?" I asked. She stared at the bill. I knew what was racing through her head. How many dicks was she going to have to suck, how much abuse was she going to have to suffer to get that money for answering one question. I'm sure she began to see glimpses of the past horrors of her life for even what she had been through, as tough as a whore as she must be. She began to sob.

She reached for the bill. "Sixteen," she blurted.

I got up quickly and dressed. I could see the whole scenario playing in my mind, "AMERICAN EXECUTIVE ARRESTED WITH CHILD. JUDGE SEEKS MOLESTATION CHARGE!" I kissed her as tenderly as possible on the forehead and once on the lips, and left. To her, I was just another gringo John who has yet to learn the realities of life; way down south of the border. To me, she was a tragedy of mankind, but right now, I wanted to murder Wally for he knew this all long before we set off. What did he want? There were no pictures, just stories. Contract security, perhaps? I was not in control of his business future. I just was certain there had to be a motive. Uncle Wally was a pisshead, yes, but he was a slick, crafty old bastard. I found the Madam and she brought me to the gaudy, brocade sin bin Wally had reposted to for the evening. She opened the door with the master key and there was Wally, looking like a bloated whale sandwich between two slices of brown bread. He was startled.

"Grab your clothes," I shouted. "This evening is concluded."

The girls shrieked, gathered their belongings and whatever dollars were lying about and bolted for the door. Wally was struggling to get into his trousers. He still had no idea of what the problem was. Wally bid all adieus as we rushed into the quiet dawn light. Out of breath, panting, he managed "Do you know what this evening cost me?"

"I don't care. You're billing rates are high as they are," I said. "The girl you set me up with, she was sixteen! sixteen, Wally for Christ's sake!"

"Is that it?" he said. "Is that why we ran out?"

"Yes, precisely. I can't take these risks publicly."

"For God's sake man, this is Columbia!" he said. "Get with the program, this is not Washington. Besides, they all say their sixteen or close. They think we won't want them unless they're young."

"Just get us back to the hotel and don't bring this up ever again," I said. He knew this was more than just a subtle threat. It meant money, a lot more money than Wally lost back in that whorehouse. I did keep the address however for future reference.

On another excursion into the unknown, Wally and I were due to drive to Medellín to visit a bank branch office there. Wally had been there previously and knew the road. Prior to getting into the car, he handed me a pistol.

"Here, stick this in your pants," he said.

"Why?" I asked him nervously.

"You never know. We may run into bandits on the way out there." I'd be lucky if I didn't blow my dick off with the damn thing!

Medellín was Pablo Escobar's hometown. It is a rather nice, well-kept glass and aluminum environment; absolutely the furthest thing in your mind from what you'd expect. Escobar had put some money into this town; new schools, new football fields, houses, banks, roads, you name it. To these people, he was a hero, a saint, "local boy makes good." They did not see him as a murderer. Cocaine has been in existence in this region since before Christ. Its medicinal qualities were essential to survive in the jungle. Besides, I didn't see any Walgreen's. If the stupid Americans wanted to shovel tablespoons of the shit up their noses, pussies and assholes for billions of dollars a year, that was their choice, their business, their problem. I never saw a local touch the stuff, let alone discuss it openly. Escobar was ruthless, but this was about money, nothing more, and nothing less.

There was a bounty of $1,000 for any American brought dead to the main plaza in town, training for Escobar recruits. We were off limits. They needed this technology installed to support monetary transfers offshore of the huge amounts of profit from the drug trade. Escobar trained his gunmen at age nineteen. They were instructed to go out into the night and return before morning with a body, preferably dead. Any body would do. There were no set criteria. Just bring one in, like a deer. His gunmen had a shelf life of just four years before they lost their nerve and their judgment began to falter. It was definitely a young man's world. But given an alternative, anything beat the squalor and misery surrounding them each waking day. For them and their families, it was a no lose situation. That is, unless you're shot dead.

It had been weeks in the making, but finally Uncle Wally was ready to make his pitch. Wally had made several trips to Panama City where the bank's main international branch was located. During those visits, Wally had fallen madly in love with Carmella, the branch manager. I mean love, big time; the real thing.

"You've got to put in a wire transfer system in that branch and link it to Bogotá. They desperately need it for business to carry on," he said.

"I don't have to do anything of the sort," I said. "It's not what I came here to do!"

Wally was starting to get sickening and beg. "But I promised her you would help."

"You shouldn't have. You don't even know me."

"I'm in a tough spot here," he pleaded. "I promised her you would take a look at the situation and try to help her."

"All right, all right," I said. "Get me the specifications and I'll do what I can."

"I'll owe you big time, John, big time," he said, with obvious relief.

Little did I know that "big time" was what the both of us were going to serve once this scam got out. Linking SWIFT, the international monetary transfer system, into an existing branch configuration as large as this with as many branches in many countries was not difficult in and of itself to do, and had more to do with SWIFT than us. A few programs, some test data, integration testing and a move to production, and bingo, you were in business. Wally was elated for he had made good on his promise to his sweetie and I had him off my back.

A few weeks later, I had to go to Orlando to brief a vendor on how to complete a request for proposal for a competing bank. Minutes before I arrived at the Bogotá airport, two Columbian politicians, both old friends, coincidently arrived at the airport at the same time, at opposite ends of the terminal. They had been buddies since childhood. One was now running for President, the other was the head of the Communist party. When they recognized each other, they ran toward the center of the loading area, embracing each other warmly. About mid-terminal, at that exact instant, a sedan peeled around the corner before anyone could react. The gunmen in the car sprayed bullets on everyone in sight. The soldiers accompanying the men were the first to hit the ground for cover. The two old amigos died in each other's clutches. At polar ends of the political spectrum but brothers until death did they part. The gunmen had apparently become confused over who they were supposed to kill, so they shot them both. One was a do-gooder; the other a red. No great loss from the drug trade point of view.

As this panic was ensuing outside, I was already inside, pushing to board the Miami flight and get out of there before they sealed off the airport. We just made it aloft in time. When you settle back in your seat with that inner comfort of peace and security that you're going home, it's like you've just had a good shit!

The relief to be in Orlando was overwhelming and it was to be brief. I had spent the afternoon lecturing the vendor on how winnable this business was and how to prepare the document required. He was less than convinced with my argument, having been through this before at a preparation cost of $100,000 per document, and walking with nothing more than his dick in his hand.

I liked to watch the CBS evening news with Dan Rather. It always marked the end of an arduous day, like a good martini. When Connie Chung, her of the self-invented Barbara Walter's lisp joined the team, I stopped watching. So did the rest of America. And then it came, rolling out of Dan's lips as the feature evening story. A sting operation involving five jewelry stores across the south of the United States, laundering cartel money from Columbia through to the international branch of Banco d' Occidente in Panama City and on to Bogotá! One hundred thoughts start racing through my mind and you can't connect two of them to even try to frame out a picture. First on my mind was how to tell Doug, my vendor, who had already bid this job and was coming to pick me up for dinner. After the initial shock, it became almost laughable. I dressed for dinner and stood in front of the hotel waiting. Bo Jackson, the baseball/football player, was standing there as well, looking elegant in white shorts. Bo knows. He was as big as a house. A Porsche pulled up and I watched him painfully try to stuff that frame into the tiny import. It looked like someone trying to get into a Matchbox toy. Then Doug pulled up. He took me to a local fish house. Not wanting to waste any time, I broke the news. He laughed. How funny he really thought it was I'm not certain. We made idle chitchat the rest of the evening, and he dropped me off. I never spoke to him again about this or any other deal. The next day, I flew back to Bogotá.

I decided first to seek out Jorge Morales and try to mend the fences between us, particularly in light of recent developments. He wasn't in; maybe it was fate. I saw the rest of our team who informed me I was to attend a 4:00 p.m. meeting. It was to include Jorge's assistant, Clara, who in my absence, had been promoted to a loftier position with the bank's project team. It did not go well. I managed to insult all there, particularly Clara, by staring at her and licking my lips, announcing that Jorge was an idiot and didn't know how to run a bank and telling them they owed our firm $900,000 US, not in fucking Columbian "Monopoly" money! Jamie Caro, a little worm of a man who had been stabbing me in the back every chance he got said, "You cannot speak about Jorge in this manner, he is the head of the bank!" I replied I had nothing to say and walked out. I figured it would take Clara an hour to get to Jorge and tell him what I said. I didn't care anymore. It was obvious to me everyone was on the take from day one; that it was a set-up and they never had any intentions of paying our bill to begin with. The local partner, a Korean (you figure it out, I couldn't), hadn't even sent a single invoice the entire year that the team had been there. I just wished I had one shot at giving Clara a private tutorial in colonic purging; she has an ass just built for it!

I went stalking Uncle Wally. I found him right where I knew I would. Surprisingly, he was sober as a judge.

"I made a tragic mistake, and at my age," he sputtered.

"You could not have known," I replied. "Women are intoxicating at any age." It was of little solace, but it was all I could offer.

"Wally, no one will ever know the reason," I continued. "It was a noble gesture. I don't shoot good men. We'll deal with it if we are confronted. Besides, they made a legitimate request for the service to be built. But right now, I've got to find Cliff."

I went straight to my apartment. Cliff was already sitting there. The maid let him in. Great security I thought.

Cliff was ten years my junior and a nicer guy you wouldn't want to meet. He was a Jew, but I don't think anyone told him that. The way fate goes we would be together years later in Munich where he was best man at my wedding. He had worked this project hard for nine months. He was worn. He looked like most expats in this country.

Cliff was very nervous. Cliff was always nervous. Maybe it was because he didn't get laid enough or when he did, he suffered from

Jewish guilt because if he didn't propose to the girl, it reduced her to a slut in his mind. We once sent him to Hawaii for R & R from a job in New Zealand; a much laid back place, because of stress. On this particular day, he was sweating profusely.

"John, I don't know quite how to put this, but Jorge wants you out of here," he began apologetically.

"I'm not surprised after that meeting," I said.

"You don't understand," he continued. "He wants you out of here like now, as in tonight." His face tightened.

"Well, let's go to the office and call Cathy. It's early enough. Maybe she could do her thing." She couldn't, it would have to wait until very early the next morning. Our female staff, Christy and Sara, was visibly upset. The door opened and in came Uncle Wally, remarkably for this time of the evening, still sober.

"Do you think Jorge will send someone to kill you," he asked. The girls freaked.

"Well Wally, by all general appearances, I suspect that's crossed their minds," I replied.

"Can't we hide you anywhere?" Christy asked.

"Then I run the risk of being gunned down on the street. No, it's too risky, there is no safe place," I said.

"We have to keep moving around as much of the night as possible, stay visible, lots of witnesses," Wally said. "They may think twice because you're an American. Heck, it's worth a try, nothing to lose!"

Wally was right. It's harder to hit a moving target than a stationary one. And move we did. From restaurant to bar, bar to apartment, apartment to coffee shop and back to bar. Most of this I did with Wally. It became more precarious and limited as curfew crept upon us. We finally ended up back at my apartment. It was around midnight. I had already packed what I intended taking.

"Wait here, I'll be right back," Wally said. He returned a few minutes later with a bulge in his shirt. He took a chair and placed it about seven feet back from the door.

"Here, take this," he said.

It was the gun he had previously given me on our trip to Medellín.

"You may only get off a shot or two, but if that's all they send, you're in business. If the first guy is the shooter, you'll hear them try to open the door. They're real dumb fucks. Just fire through the door twice. If there's more than one shooter, you're dead!" Wally was scared shitless, but he was he was trying to act real tough.

"Listen," he said. "There's only three hours left before you have to leave to go to the airport and no one's shown up yet. If there are no holes in the door at 5:00 a.m. precisely, open it up." He disappeared down the long, musky hallway into the darkness.

Up to this point, I was about to begin what was left of the most terrifying night of my life. I dimmed the lights and unlocked the safety of the revolver. The gun was old but clean, in good working condition. My father taught me a lot about guns and shooting. My grandfather had been a chief of police, so there were always guns around the house and men wearing them. My father was a champion shot in his day. I sat down in the chair with the gun at my side.

I heard a noise outside. *Do I start blasting and turn this entire complex upside down, or wait?* I thought to myself, *patience.* Then another thud. I held up the gun at mid-chest level and took aim at the door. It was now 4:00 a.m., perfect time for a murder. No fiddling of the doorknob yet. I decided to end the suspense. I got up out of the line of fire and moved sideways toward the door. I heard mumbling outside. I held the .45 firmly with both hands, like I'd been taught, prepared to pivot and fire. Another thud. I slid sideways to look in the peephole of the door. Not surprising, it was Manny the night watchman, drunk as a skunk, bouncing off the walls, talking to himself. I had to fart, but held it in fearing it would be of the liquid variety. I returned to my post. I know I dozed off a few times for my head bounced, like when you have an aisle seat in a plane. It was becoming daybreak, 4:45 a.m. I went in the bathroom and washed my face and hands. I was dressed in leather pants, a leather jacket and boots. It hadn't even occurred to me to wear a suit. 4:55 a.m. I shut off the light and waited a five-minute eternity. At exactly 5:00, I opened the door as Wally had instructed me to do. It was difficult to believe what I saw. Standing there was Uncle Wally with a hotel laundry basket on rollers, filled with sheets, shirts, etc. He was dressed in white hotel coveralls that said "Estaban" where your gas station attendant's name appears. He had a flat cap pulled down over his head. He threw me a similar pair of coveralls.

"Put these on and get in, cover yourself up," he instructed. Mine said "Enrico" on them. I don't know how he did it, but they fit perfectly.

After looking at me in my leather outfit, he said, "Christ, you look more like a drug dealer than they do!"

I got in with my sack and covered myself up. "There may be problems," he said. "The guard shift has just changed." He pushed us to the service elevator. It seemed like forever until the *ping* of its arrival sounded. Wally pushed us over the lip and the door closed behind. The old man was in good shape despite all the sauce he poured into himself daily. When the elevator halted, we were in the basement. "Get out," he commanded.

I climbed out from the shit and menstrual-stained linens and we were standing face to face. He smiled for the first time in two days.

"Head for the back of the hotel," he said. "I'll direct you. I know most of the passages because I fuck most of the girls at the front desk down here. Can't bring them to the room; too risky. If anyone confronts you, don't speak. Don't shoot either. I'll handle this."

We wove a trail through the twisting corridors filled with boiler pipes, debris, empty booze bottles, just an assortment of shit. One bellboy walked by; he just nodded. It was still early, at least in Columbia. I turned my head and saw the dawn at the door. As corny as it sounds, it was the light at the end of the tunnel. There was one body lying there. It was not a Columbian, but a white-skinned gringo. Another deal gone bad? Wrong target again? Or was it just the beginning of another typical day in Bogotá?

"Get out of the coveralls," Wally ordered. He seemed to be acting out of a single mindedness of purpose to get me out of Columbia alive or maybe he just didn't want to appear before a Senate subcommittee probing the laundering scam. There was a car waiting. We stripped down out of the hotel coveralls. Wally was in a jacket and tie.

Bogotá was serenely quiet at this hour of the morning. There were a few cars, some locals with burros walking alongside the road, just your basic peasantry. The driver dumped us at the airport terminal. It too was very quiet. No one had followed us. Uncle Wally took me to the counter and in Spanglish, checked me in. We had a brief cup of coffee in the canteen.

"Well, kid, this is all I can do for you. You're on your own with the soldiers in there. I have no idea what will happen. I'm sorry for what I caused," he offered.

"Just tell Cliff to get the money those pricks owe us," I told him. "If not, his career is history! Goodbye, Wally," I said.

I slowly headed for security. I turned around to see Wally's face pressed to the glass. I knew he was shitting. They stamped my passport easily enough which meant I was legally free to go. They would have to find a way to nail me in customs.

The sergeant in charge was a large, fat unshaven pig, just like the bumbling fool in the Zorro TV series, Sergeant Garcia. He was the one Zorro always used to carve a "Z" across his belly. He stunk of bad whiskey, BO, and stale pussy. He had a few of his minions standing around, one of whom frisked me rather slowly. I thought, *Oh no, next comes the free proctoscopy exam courtesy of the Columbian army!* It didn't happen. They searched the bag and found nothing. Then the sergeant moved closer and suddenly became arrogant. I didn't understand a word he said. Wally was clawing at the glass but everyone just ignored him. The sergeant unstrapped his holster and withdrew his gun. He put it to my temple. My arms were shuddering. He asked me another question in Spanish and I answered in Spanish, the little I understood. The guards laughed. In the sentence, I heard him mention the words, *la coca*, which means "the cocaine," as opposed to just *coca*, which refers to the American national beverage, Coca Cola. He then grabbed my nose hard and bent it from side to side, I'm assuming to see if my nostrils were inflamed and would begin bleeding, a sure sign of cocaine use. They didn't. He took the barrel of his gun, pulled back my waistband and stuck the end in. Just what I wanted, to be a eunuch for the rest of my life! Again, he shouted the same question. I responded with the same answer, "*No la coca!*" He then spied something I had hoped would interest him more. I had gone "New York" on him while I was in the bathroom of the coffee shop. I had taken a new, crisp one hundred dollar bill and put it in my pants pocket with just enough of the tip showing, but not enough that he could tell the denomination. I had my hands up in the air. He looked at me smiling, rotten teeth and all. I was going to gamble and play the only card I had. He slowly slipped the bill out and as the denomination appeared, he yanked the gun from my trousers, put the bill in the palm of his hand and straightened out my jacket.

"My amigo, *por favor!*" he said with a broad sweeping gesture of his arm. I swore to myself I would have killed this cocksucker had we been in a different circumstance.

I boarded the Avianca flight to Miami, which at that hour was empty. When we landed in Florida, it was a different story. Flights had arrived from all over Latin and South America. Hundreds of people were fighting over luggage carts, boxes tied with rope, you name it and all over the place, US Marshals with annoying, drug sniffing little dogs climbing all over everyone. I said to myself, "There is no way"; as I had a connecting flight to North Carolina with a two-hour window in between, usually plenty of time to make it. It took over one hour just to make it to immigration.

Cliff told me to tell the immigration service that I was in Bogotá visiting a friend since we had been working in Columbia the entire duration without work permits. The Immigration Officer asked me what I did for a living and I said I was a consultant. He looked at me in my leather pants and asked what I was doing in Bogotá.

"Visiting a friend," I replied.

Did I speak Spanish?

"A little," I said.

He asked me to count to ten. I got to three but told him my friend spoke Spanish fluently. He told me to go to Area Three. I was really shitting now not from the hassle, but from the fact that I was going to miss my plane and would have to hang out in Miami for hours.

There were three young men from the Dominican Republic ahead of me being hassled by INS officers. These kids were so drunk it was really a comedy to watch them. They also stunk very badly. They were trying to bring in more than their allotted quota of rum. They had the stuff in paper bags, not their suitcases. One of the bags broke and a quart of it went careening to the floor, smashing all over the place, showering everyone in the vicinity with liquor. They were so out of it they were "Detained" for being undesirable. It was sad in a way but this was three less people my tax money was going to have to support in welfare payments and eventually, jail.

Then they got around to me. The officer asked me what I was doing in Columbia, speaking in a deep Southern drawl. This time I told him the truth. He asked me where I was going and I said North Carolina.

"Where in North Carolina," he wanted to know.

"A small town twenty miles out of Raleigh that wasn't even on the map," I replied.

"I'm from those parts, try me," he said, becoming excited at the prospect.

"A little place called New Hill," I said.

"Well heck," he exclaimed. "I'm from just down the road a lick in Moncure!"

He gave me a big country bear hug. I felt like fucking Opie and Gomer from the Andy Griffith Show. Moncure was such an exciting place I used to drive around there with my girlfriend at night, the both of us half naked, drinking cheap wine, just to see if anyone would notice. They never did. He asked to see one of my business cards just for validity's sake.

"Why did they send you to see me?" he asked inquisitively.

"Heck if I know," I mustered in my best Carolina drawl, which at best was pretty bad.

"Well, you best hurry up or ya'll miss that plane," he said, waving for the crowd to part like Moses and the Red Sea.

I did make it with a minute or so to spare. On the way home on the puddle jumper, I thought what a fiasco this whole assignment had been. We never, to no one's surprise, did any more work for the bank again. We never had to testify about our wrong doings. We did eventually collect the money they owed us and I did catch a bucket of shit from my superiors. And what about Uncle Wally? Well they just don't make them like him anymore!

You may ask does Columbia have to do with Iraq. As ill-prepared as I was for this adventure, it was just a small indication of the things yet to come!

CHAPTER 2

Baghdad by the Bay

I'm confused! Herb Caen, the late revered sage of the *San Francisco Chronicle* always referred to his city as "Baghdad by the Bay." Maybe this is some analogy to the days of sin and debauchery alleged to have existed in ancient Baghdad. Today, those sins are minimally punished by death. Perhaps the fable "Ali Baba and the Forty Thieves" was what he had in mind. There is a corroded bronze monument to the tale in the middle of a traffic round about in Baghdad central. For the British rebuilt this city after 400 years of the Ottoman Empire with the same city planners they used in every other city they occupied, replete with circuitous, nonsensical roads from Auckland to Riyadh to London. They're all the same no matter what part of the world you are in. Ever wonder why things are so fucked up in the Middle East? The British Empire is the answer. Churchill and Lawrence of Arabia drew lines and said, "Iraq is as good a name as you'll find for this land mass! Call it Iraq, pick out a local and install him as King, have another Pimms No. 6 Cup and let's get the hell out." Everywhere they went; Burma, India, and South Africa and on, it was all the same legacy. They haven't recovered from the sectarian violence in three generations nor will we ever be free from it here in the States. It will never have an end. Next, the Arabs will be fighting over Camden, New Jersey, and other garden spots from which to build fundamentalist cells from. Let me provide you with a few useful travel tips should the need ever arise in your lifetime to visit Iraq.

Getting Prepared

I knew I was in trouble when I popped into my favorite book-store in Georgetown and did not find a copy of Fodor's *Let's Have Fun in Iraq*. Don't bring anything of value or that you value. The Iraqi's are not murderers, child molesters, or rapists. They are just dirt poor. They will steal anything that is not nailed down. When you go through customs, they will look at any alcohol you bring in and say, "Oh, this bottle must be for me!" and take your liquor so that you're reduced to drinking Jordanian gin, which has a similar consistency to paint remover. They will remove your camera batteries so nothing can be photographed. They will write the room number in your hotel in ballpoint ink on the inside label of your jacket or trousers to remember whom it belongs to. After several hotels, my clothes resembled a bookmaker at Belmont racetrack with all the var-ious numbers written inside. My first day at the Al-Rasheed Hotel, they stole my Sony Walkman and onyx cufflinks. Other than that, they are a fun bunch of people!

Getting There

I loved standing on the tarmac at Zürich Airport, freezing to death in single file waiting to board a British Trident jet from the rear of the plane. It does wonders for your tinnitus standing under roaring jet engines. This is all so you can be body searched by hand for the third time. Iraq's are basically cowards as the Gulf War proved. They just like feeling your balls! When you are flying at night, the period in which most flights originate and depart from Baghdad, one can-not help but being awed by an incredible light emanating from about fifty miles from Baghdad. It looks like the set to *Close Encounters of the Third Kind* or a well-lit baseball stadium in the States; if you could see through the pollution. Quite eerie and mysterious.

Iraqi Airways went downhill after Saddam decided he fancied the President of the airlines' blonde-haired wife as his paramour. As a gesture of goodwill, he let the guy live. Iraqi Airways also bought the hotel Le Meridian from the French and turned it into the Palestine Hotel. Within a month, the place was crawling with cockroaches.

Leaving Iraq

If you are an Iraqi citizen, you cannot. They are virtually prisoners in the country with little exception other than the well-connected few. If you hold a resident permit, you cannot leave without police approval. My friend and colleague, Tony L. ran the defense systems for the government. He was not permitted to leave at the outbreak of Desert Shield. They beat him mercilessly. He was never the same again in his life; more like a walking zombie. As a "reward" when all was over, his company assigned him to the island of Malta to run their operations there, a place where he didn't have to think too much. He was virtually incapable of it regardless.

The Iran-Iraq War

History repeats itself, always. We Americans just can't seem to grasp this concept. As detailed later in this book, Saddam fought this war not just for Iraq, but also for the entire Arab world and contained Islamic fundamentalism from the soft, Muslim underbelly of the then Soviet Union. Ironically, this is the primary reason George Bush left him in power instead of taking him down. Eight years, one million soldiers from sides, one million civilian deaths, scores maimed for life. In the last battle, which was our equivalent of Gettysburg, soldiers' taped plastic keys to their foreheads? If they died in battle, the key would unlock the gates to heaven. In a slaughter, the Iraqis lost 50,000 boys. The whole war ended in a stalemate; an undeclared truce. The day of the Kuwait invasion, Mr. Abdullah, the bank's project manager, said to me that he would see us again. I looked at him like he was nuts, as I frantically tried to get out of the building which was across the street from the Ministry of Defense, a target that I expected at any minute would be slammed by a US cruise missile. I stopped to ask him what he meant, as ludicrous as it sounded to me. He said they had survived an eight-year war with Iran, then pumped their way out of it into the black, that with patience, this upcoming conflict would have an end as well. The funny thing is, the bugger is probably right!

The Regime

I think no one put it better than Tariq Aziz, the wily, old diplomat who was the Deputy Minister of Foreign Affairs, when he said, "We have been in power too long!" And he is right. Saddam's Baath splinter group has been in control of the country from 1958 until today. That's a long, damn time in anybody's book. Now, Tariq is tired. He is a Christian and a grandfather. During one visit to the United Nations, US Ambassador Madeline Albright gave him exactly two minutes of her precious time in a hallway. Personally, I think she's a guy. I conveyed a message to Tariq via an intermediary to reach under her skirt to and see if there's a cock hanging there! I'm certain there is. Tariq's New York doctor told him he was on the verge of a stroke and suffering from clinical depression. I wonder if *Listening to Prozac?* had been published in Arabic. Tariq also talks frequently of committing suicide.

Of the nine men ruling junta, five are Muslim and four are Christian. My boss in Baghdad, Dr. Mohammed Saleh, then Minister of Finance, is a graduate of the University of Michigan. I once did a presentation before him and fifty shuddering members of the Rasheed Bank at gunpoint. The bankers started muttering amongst themselves. Dr. Saleh turned on the couch and said, "He is an American, speak English, I know you can all speak English!" And they could, fluently, for it is a mandate to graduate from school. How many languages does your kid speak? The regime built highways, schools, universities, hospitals, and shopping centers. They united a warring, nomadic group of tribes under one strongman. They built mosques. They allowed Christianity to grow. There is even a Jewish population of 3,500 people in Baghdad with a temple. I know their accountant; he took me there. The Jews donate a lot of money to the regime.

The regime also murdered many people for a multitude of reasons. The amount is probably incalculable. They are getting old and tired and are making more mistakes. But they are preparing for a whole new group to step in, including Saddam's murderous sons, who control the national press, TV and the secret police. Law requires a picture of Saddam every ten feet. Saddam in military garb, white dinner jacket, desert warrior, you name it. The same personality cult created by Nasser, Assad, Khadafy and Khomeni. Can the sons' keep it going to a next generation? The world and the Iraqi people hope not.

Saddam Election Day

I must be one of few Americans ever to publicly witness the seven-year term presidential election of Saddam Hussein. I was "invited," also meaning made to go, along with my colleague, Christy Compton, who I first met in Bogotá as detailed in the previous chapter. Christy was a knockout with natural curly, strawberry blonde hair, green eyes, and the greatest set of legs I've ever seen on a woman. I had the hots for her real bad, but then so did everyone else. Except everyone else wasn't her boss. Christy was from Oklahoma and a little, let's say "dingy." She still referred to her boyfriends as "beaus" while I crudely referred to woman as "broads." We were herded into a large hall within the bank containing row after row of folding chairs. It also had long tables covered with plates of various sweets, cakes, candy, etc. After being seated, a woman from the Baath party stepped up to the podium and reading from a prepared text, extolled the virtues of Saddam's accomplishments, or so I was told. After every break in the text, the bank personnel applauded and the women broke out into a high, ululating shrill. A plate of some gelatin-like candy, covered in powdered sugar was being passed around and we were told to eat a piece. It was awful. I just swallowed mine whole and tried not to think about what it was. I hoped maybe it was hash oil, but it tasted more like motor oil. Christy looked at me like a little kid and said, "I don't like it, what should I do with it?" I had to give her my clean, silk handkerchief; she faked a cough and spit it out, then handed it back to me. More speeches. Finally, the last speaker whipped the crowd into frenzy, all hell broke loose and people started chanting, "Saddam, Saddam!" which I surmised was an overwhelming "Yes" ballot. Then they charged for the sweet table and devoured it. Then, as many as could, crowded toward open windows, still shouting and ululating, throwing confetti out the window into the street below. All the buildings along Haifa Street did the same. It was a ticker tape parade except for one, minor detail. There was no parade, no floats, no marching bands, and no hero in an open car. There was only the rancid stench of the sewer floating upward. Abruptly, everyone went back to work. That's it, seven more years of tyranny. It was one of the few dank, overcast days I encountered in my tenure there. Maybe on such an auspicious day, it served as an indication of what was to soon come.

The Rasheed Bank

Our client. I will not bore you with the workings of the bank because this bank is just as fucked up as the bank you and I bank with in the free world with one exception; being in this bank was more akin to being in a Fellini movie. It was so unique it was almost an art form. The bank was run by Majid Al-Ani, an older, short grandfatherly type and Saddoun Kubba, his henchman and Chief of Operations. It was rumored that over the many years they controlled the bank, they had each ferreted away about $80 million in foreign currency into numbered accounts in Switzerland. The bank performed an audit once a year, in December, which literally gave you eleven months to steal as much as you could and cover it up. When we performed an audit, we discovered amongst other things that billions of cash was missing, vanished without a trace. When we informed bank officials in a presentation, they just laughed. We eventually tracked the missing cash. It was simply scattered amongst 500 branches and just unaccounted for. Tellers who made the equivalent of $100 a month were covered in gold bracelets and rings. This just didn't click. One afternoon, we followed the chief cashier in a downtown branch home. We hung back far enough not to be noticed. In about three blocks, she climbed into a brand new Mercedes Benz 300 E! On $100 a month salary? I don't think so. The thievery was rampant and with no real accurate records, untraceable.

They took us to visit a "typical" branch. It was like traveling back in time. Inside the three stories building was a staircase going up to the top floor. Up and down both sides of it were Egyptian workers waiting to transfer money home to their relatives in Cairo and elsewhere. The heat and the stench were unbearable. "How long do they wait?" I asked our guide.

"Sometimes all day," he said.

"What do they do if they run out of time and the branch closes?" I said.

"They just come back the next day and resume their place in line until they reach the teller line," he answered.

"Does the money ever get there?" I asked honestly.

"Sometimes," he said matter-of-factly. Your chances of getting a letter through to Santa Claus were better! Later on in my stay, I had a young Egyptian man plead with me to help them find the money they sent that never arrived or send it for them. Now I knew where all the Mercedes were coming from.

I often noticed a fine dirt powder in my pants pockets and on my hands at the end of the day. Whenever I fingered cash, there was always a reddish, sandy substance on the bills, but I could never figure out what it was and why it was always there.

In the branch, I saw burlap bags the size of fertilizer bags you buy in the hardware store piled one on top of the other to about four feet high. From the bottom of the bags, water was oozing out onto the marble floor forming a puddle that everyone just walked thru.

"What's in those bags?" I asked.

"Money," was the response.

"Why is it wet?" I pressed on.

"Because it's just been washed," they answered.

"Where and how? I wanted to know as I was totally intrigued with what the answer would be.

"By being dragged through the Tigris River and left to dry."

That explained the fine residue on the bills. It was silt stirred up from the bottom of the river. It also explained why the money was often damp and smelled musty. It gave a whole new meaning to "laundering money!"

The Information Technology department was no better off. Faxes were illegal except where they could be monitored by the government. Telephone communications was a disaster. You never knew who was listening in. The entire data center was in danger of fire due to an aging, failing public telephone switchboard machine in the basement, covered in grease and oil. Hussein (no relation to Saddam) the technology department manager, came running after me frantically one morning. He was still on reserve duty from the Army. He had the Minister of Finance on the telephone that wanted to know how many of the 10,000 Olivetti terminals he had ordered did I want.

I said, "None." Hussein turned ashen.

"You can't say that," he blurted out.

"Sure I can," I said. "I have no idea of what my requirements will be."

I knew the position he was in. He was now cold sweating, but I wanted him to experience the moment so he knew who was really in charge. He was probably thinking this was his ticket back to the Iranian front lines."

I said, "Tell him a number that suits you."

He dashed back to the phone. We figured it was all kickback money for the Ministry and the terminals hadn't even left the dock in Genoa yet. Security was a farce. It consisted of one old man who was usually asleep on the couch in the lobby every day when we left. He always had a kerchief bundled up in front of him. One afternoon, I took it and opened it up. Inside was a revolver. The barrel was bent to the left. I wondered if he could shoot around corners with it. I covered it up and left him in peace.

Baghdad at Night

No doubt about it, a very swinging place. When the war with Iran began, most daytime activity was curtailed for fear of a missile attack. Miraculously, only one missile struck downtown, demolishing a building you could have knocked down by farting. So on daytime plane flights, no Iraqi citizen was allowed to leave the country and most retail businesses closed during the day. The Iraqis' grew quite accustomed to this schedule. When the war ended and the country reverted back to daylight hours, Baghdad became one big K-Mart, open twenty-four hours a day, seven days a week. Subsequently, daytime and nighttime became transparent. You could get a haircut and a shave at 3:00 a.m. or 3:00 p.m. You could shop for vegetables at 11:00 a.m. or 11:00 p.m. and on and on it went. Nightclubs and discos abounded. The local whiskey was diabolical, but if you could afford it, foreign whiskey was available.

Iraqis are an open, friendly people and naturally curious, particularly of Americans and American habits. While we sat and ate dinner one night at the Sheraton Hotel, hordes of Iraqis poured in like an endless parade. When they reached the end of the lobby, they would make a U-turn and file back out again. I asked the manager of the hotel what they were so curious about.

"Oh, nothing in particular," he said. "They just wanted to see what was going on."

The Al-Rasheed Hotel

The diplomatic "in-spot" to be. Always, day and night, a parking lot filled with officialdom. It was rumored Saddam had his bunker headquarters built underneath the hotel. Before Desert Shield was staged, he moved all the hostages into the hotel so the allies wouldn't bomb it. It was not under the hotel. I was under the hotel. Every floor is segmented by nationality; Americans on one, French on another, Germans on another and so on and so forth. Under the hotel was a huge listening post, monitoring all telephone traffic. The floors were segmented by language because it made wire-tapping and translation easier!

Ordering breakfast was one of my favorite times of the day. When you requested a soft-boiled egg, you got fried. An omelet, you got poached; scrambled, you got, well, it could be anything. Our team fought with the waiter's daily until we developed a system. Just order anything at all and when it arrived, switch your order with another member who had what you wanted. Soon, we taught all the hotel guests the same system. The National Restaurant was good until Saddam's son, Udai, began using it as his gangster get together spot. He was a psychopathic murder; the scariest man I have ever met in my life and possibly the next Iraqi leader. It had a pretty good bar scene if drinking was your thing.

Egyptian Airport Terminal

Hosni Mubarak, the Egyptian President, paid a visit to Saddam one year before the start of the Muslim holy month of Ramadan. Thousands of Egyptians were returning home to observe it or making the pilgrimage to Mecca, known as the Haj. Upon Mubarak's departure, his car drove past these thousands of his countrymen at the airport waiting in a single line to get on a flight out. You dare not leave your place in line for if you did, you went to the back of the line and started all over again, making this process take days before you could get on a plane. Therefore, the Egyptians ate, slept, shit, and pissed in the same spot. Picture this in the broiling sun! Egyptians were considered "guest workers," like the Turks in Germany not to be treated with the same privileges as an Iraqi. They were actually treated lower than dirt. Mubarak was enraged. By the time of his next visit, Saddam had built the Egyptians their own terminal.

The Baghdad Observer

A great little paper printed daily in English except Saturday. This newspaper was key to understanding what the regime was plotting. For instance, if it stated that metal pipes sent to Baghdad were for an oil pipeline, not to build the alleged "Supergun," you just reversed the headline to get the true meaning. That's exactly what they were building was the gun, not the pipeline. When the British sent a smelter for titanium production, not plutonium, that's exactly what the regime wanted it for, bomb building. It also carried news of executions and American baseball scores.

Babylon

One of the great disappointments in my life! One of the seven wonders of the world and here I was, at the doorstep of The Tower of Babel. I could barely contain my excitement. We rented a car and driver and set out on a blistering hot day. The ride was about 120 miles or so south of Baghdad. The terrain was almost completely barren save for a small village and a factory of some kind, most likely clinker, used in the manufacture of concrete. I slept a bit and listened to the radio. Finally, the driver pulled off the main highway and down a paved, black top road, lined on both sides with tall, date filled palm trees. The grass surrounding the area was as green as Ireland. We pulled into the parking lot and bought tickets. There was an amphitheater off to one side. I envisioned seeing "A Night Under the Stars-The Who at the Tower of Babel." The Who and Roger Daltrey singing "We Won't Get Fooled Again." What an appropriate song for Iraq! It was all heady stuff and then we saw what remains of Babylon. It was literally just an excavated pit, a dirt hole, nothing more than a series of disjointed walls having no relation to anything whatsoever. Its composition was dusty red clay. I remember saying to no one in particular; "this is the extent of what they've done for history since they seized power?" I walked town a tar path to what remains of the Tower of Babel. All that is there are two tiers and very undistinguish-able at that. It was a bummer of historical proportions. Being totally disgusted, I hit the souvenir shop and started back toward the car. I was also quite pissed because this little junket had cost us $300 dollars! And then, I saw him. A motorcade had entered the grounds, black Mercedes Benzes all over the place. Standing amongst a group of soldiers was none other than Saddam Hussein himself! I wanted to go over and talk to him, tell him who I was and what I was doing for his country. I wanted to tell him he needed the Disney people real bad down in this shit pit of an attraction. As I moved toward his direction I heard the safety come off a dozen rifles. I stopped in my tracks and went quietly back to the car.

The only other symbol of national pride was a downed Iranian fighter smashed to bits on the front lawn of what used to be the old

US embassy building. There is a story behind the plane and its pilot, but I can't remember it. I think the Iraqi who downed it was killed as well and was a national martyr. They probably made the whole thing up. It makes for good public relations.

The Neat Freak

Saddam was a neat freak. Baghdad is ancient, but is it very clean. They even sweep the median of the highways by hand. Saddam was visiting the governor of a southern province. He got up out of the meeting and went in to use the rest room. When he finished his business, he reached for a hand towel behind him. The towel was soiled. Saddam went nuts. The governor was only fired. He was lucky.

The Kurds

The Kurds will replace the Palestinians as the next displaced peoples of the world. It doesn't seem to matter to anyone; they have no homeland anyway. Therefore, they have no oil or so it was thought. Why would we ever get involved with a race that has nothing to offer? Like what happened in Bosnia? Why worry about human rights? There really isn't any. The United States has many versions of the definition of democracy. We just use the one that's most suited to the material objective we have in mind. Just ask Daw Aung San Sui Kyi in Burma what her definition of democracy is. I'm certain you will find it to be vastly different that the policy makers in Washington. Why risk a confrontation with the Chinese when Burma doesn't have anything our economy depends on? Even a Nobel Peace prize winner couldn't get us involved in the middle of the desperate situation in Burma.

Close Encounters of the Fourth Kind

You're probably asking, "He forgot to explain about the illuminating, mysterious glow emanating out of Baghdad at night." If you get a taxi at night and head out of the airport, you first drive past miles of a concrete anti-tank barrier. As you near the Al-Rasheed Hotel, the lights get brighter. There you discover the source of the mystery. It is a massive park, illuminated all night long, and dedicated to the veterans who died in the Iran-Iraq war. It is so bright inside that you can read a newspaper by the light. On either end of the park are enormous bronzes casts of a forearm and a hand (Saddam's), reaching skyward. They are each holding sabers that cross in the middle. You walk through these to enter the park. Around the hands are nets holding the helmets of Iranian soldiers killed in the battles. Each net contains approximately half a million helmets. There is a huge stadium, primarily used to stage tributes to the glory of Saddam Hussein. There is also a grotto with an eternal flame as a tribute to the Unknown Soldier. The grounds cover hundreds of acres and are beautifully maintained. And like most wars, it was utterly useless. George Bush left Saddam in control as a balance of power in the Middle East, essential to the future stability of the region, a counter force to the expansion of Islamic fundamentalism into the remainder of the Arab world and protection for the second largest deposit of oil known to mankind. A gangster with a bunch of hoods who effect financial markets worldwide, shift the global economy, throw terror into the lives of millions and could force the mobilization of thousands of military personnel all over the world with one idiotic statement.

Norman Schwarzkopf Jr., for wanting to go the distance, for being all that you could be, I salute you!

CHAPTER 3

"Let's Make a Deal"

Dr. Hans Knobel took me to dinner to what was one of the finest meals I've ever had in Europe. The weather at night in Zürich in June was delightful, with a mild soothing breeze coming off the lake. We started with the house specialty; small ravioli cooked to perfection, stuffed with fish mousseline in a light wine sauce. Next was sautéed veal in a brown sauce and rösti, a Swiss fried potato served with almost everything at every meal. Hans drank a sufficient amount of various wines. We had two servings of the main course, as is the Swiss custom with most anything you eat. Since I don't drink, Hans finished off the meal with Grappa, both his and mine. The bill was $400 dollars!

The restaurant was glittered from all the crystal and diamonds in the room. The air was rich with the aroma of Cuban cigars. Waiters were stepping on the bottoms of fur coats draped over the chairs, flowing onto the floor. The tables were close and as one would expect in Switzerland, the talk was mostly of money, banks, exchanges, and swindles.

Dr. Knobel was our firm's representative to the European Common Market. He was bespectacled and looked like Heinrich Himmler. He was cold and he was powerful.

"So I understand you have a desire to work for a European company, perhaps like Nestlé?" he began.

"Yes, that's my ultimate goal," I responded, knowing fully that this was a pre-rehearsed play put on by a Swiss colleague of mine who offered to be an intermediary between us.

"I know many well placed people within companies through-out Europe. Perhaps I could be of some assistance?" he said, leaning back in his chair. I had been wondering all long what the price of his assistance was going to be.

"A colleague of mine's son is the captain of the Greek National football squad," Knobel began. "He approached me with a deal where the Greek government wants to buy large quantities of oil, but not on the open market set at OPEC prices. The government has been in a cash poor situation ever since the colonel's coup and their supply of capital is very limited. We believe Saddam Hussein is in a similar situation due to the debt burden of the war with Iran and may be willing to over pump his limits and undercut his crude price to try to recoup the losses faster."

"You're talking a black market sale, Dr. Knobel," I said rather nervously.

"No, not exactly. Just a very private one," he replied rather coldly.

"For arranging this with contacts we know you have in Baghdad, you would not even need a job after the commission you would receive from a sale of this magnitude."

"But I know nothing about the oil business," I said.

"That may be true," he implied. "But you know people in Iraq who do. If it isn't feasible, I'll still get you what you want in Europe," he concluded.

Why I thought he was lying, I wasn't sure, maybe just intuition. He insisted we keep this as private as possible. He paid the bill, we extended best wishes and he promptly departed.

I walked around the block several times just inhaling the lake air, for soon I would be back to the choking oven of pollution in Baghdad. I kept asking myself how do you pull something like this off, keep it from our firm and stash the commission, not to mention stay alive to spend it. I retired to my hotel room without any answers, but with plenty of questions.

Upon returning to Baghdad, armed with only the fragment of information Dr. Knobel gave me, I started at the most logical place I knew. Farqad (picture John Rhys Davies) ran a small but successful accounting firm in Baghdad. In the 1950's, his father had been the Undersecretary of State for Iraq. This made him part of a privileged family. Since his association with me, he had been appointed our local partner and through the introductions I made for him to American firms operating in Iraq, he was making a shitpile of money advising these companies on tax and accounting matters. He was truly a man who could not believe his good fortune and thanked me for it every chance he got. His long awaited ship had finally come in and he was relishing every minute of it. As I said, he was a man of good upbringing. As a boy, he had been sent to study for his certified public accountancy in England and it was there that he developed a fondness for jazz, pussy, and beer. As a result of the latter, he became a Goliath of a man at over three hundred pounds. His wife, Bessrad, ran the house, period. On Farqad's day off, he sat in his study with the headphones on, listening to jazz and drinking a case of beer. Bessrad was half-Turkish, half-Iraqi and had five sisters. Only one of them was married and lived in Germany. Bessrad was the oldest of them. If you lined them up and proceeded down the row, they just got better looking and better looking!

Farqad was forever having us to his house where the women would wait on you hand and foot. Farqad would usually get quite drunk by the end of the evening and retire to an old, upright piano where he could boogie as well as any fat man you ever saw. He was aglow with life and once paid me the greatest compliment an Arab could pay you; I was no longer a guest, I was a member of his household.

The middle sister's name was Najla. She was in her late twenties and was drop dead gorgeous with long, curly titian hair like Rita Haworth, emerald green eyes, and succulent, full lips. She was also one of the saddest people I had ever met. In the beginning, her eyes told the entire story. Over time, she opened up to me.

"I am destined to be an old maid, Mr. John," and she started to cry. "Who will have me at this age?" My heart broke for her, but

Farqad drew the line at his sisters-in-law. Bessrad may have run the house but Farqad ran the family.

The girls were very naïve and totally dependent on him. He set it up that way. Gold on an Iraqi women was a symbol of status and position. I wore a gold bracelet as a present to myself that was worth about $1000 dollars. Najla, or Naji for short, wore several bangles on each arm. They were beautiful against her olive skin.

"See, Mr. John?" she once said to me. "Your gold is not of the quality of Iraqi gold." I didn't have the heart to tell her that her bracelets were mostly a mixture of sand and only gold plated. Farqad probably bought them at the souk for a bargain price. Bessrad was trying to quietly push a romance between us, but although Farqad loved me like a brother, he was not going to allow the best thing that ever happened to his business to get distracted by a woman, particularly under his own roof!

"Oil!" Farqad exclaimed. "Jesus Christ John, are you kidding?"

I knew this was serious shit, but just how so was yet to be known. Farqad threw everyone out of his office and began checking, as was his usual habit, for listening devices under the seat cushions, desk, etc.

"Will you relax," I said. "This request came from the Swiss."

"You can't be too certain these days," he said. "The secret police are everywhere."

"How many barrels in total?" he wanted to know. I told him I had no idea and he would just have to wait for Dr. Knobel to contact me again.

In a few short weeks, I was back in Switzerland. I don't think I could have survived the ordeal in Iraq if it wasn't for these brief respites. Dr. Knobel was waiting for me.

"How many barrels did you say again?" I asked him.

"One billion," he replied coolly. I honestly had no reaction for I had no idea what that entailed.

"One billion over one year and it must remain strictly confidential. The Greeks will finance the operation entirely through Zürich. You must tell us how much you need, when, and where," he said.

Numbers were now beginning to recoil around my head.

Knobel continued in his arrogant style. "You will be responsible personally for all the arrangements. Any loss and it's yours. If the news leaks, we will deny any complicity, understood?"

"What guarantee do I have I will get my job in Europe," I asked innocently enough.

"My dear fellow, as I said at dinner, with the commission you will make from this sale, you will never have to worry about working again, for anyone, anywhere." He was angered at my distrust of him.

It was no doubt one of the monster oil deals of all time. However, there is often great comfort in not knowing exactly how much danger you are actually in.

I flew to London and took a train to meet my parents for a brief holiday. There were some family financial matters to tend to in Bristol and then we drove up to West Kirby, not far outside of Liverpool. West Kirby, or Preston to be exact, is a quaint little seaside village of no notoriety other than being the location of John Lennon's first estate. We went to visit a retired business colleague of my father in a renovated barn that was brilliantly appointed, but freezing. I best remember them, Don and Jean for a lovely Saturday boat cruise up the Thames, in which I spent more time opening and closing river locks, a particularly precarious task when one is drunk.

Don had been head of the marine division of my father's company. He knew ships, big ships, and how to move them around the world. What luck!

"Risky business, Johnny," he began. "So many variables, so many things can go wrong."

I had given Don only a thumbnail portrait of the operation.

"First, there is acquiring a seaworthy vessel, insuring it is not pirated and what flag it is flying. It could be subject for attack for any reason, especially in the Gulf. You must have an able, experienced captain and crew, capable of warding off pirates or off-loading the cargo onto another ship and then deliberately sinking your vessel," he explained.

I was beginning to feel like I was in a cheap re-make of *Mutiny on the Bounty*! The only good news was that Marlon Brando wasn't in it.

"Then you must get the ship to the port of Basra," he continued. "This is the loading depot for oil out of Iraq, where you will more than likely be anchored for days waiting your turn to load," he said.

All in all, this conversation was becoming disheartening, as all of the aforementioned is standard operating procedure.

Don patiently continued, "The most difficult part is finding a company to reinsure the whole lot," he said.

"What exactly constitutes the whole lot," I asked him.

"There is not just the ship. piracy, cargo, crew, loading and then safe passage back to Greece," he said.

"What else could be left?" I asked.

"I believe the majority of their primary oil fields are in the west of the country? Maybe a day and a night's journey to the Gulf, yes?" he ventured.

"True," I replied.

"Well you must insure the oil being transported intact from the fields overland by trucks to the sea," he said.

"Land as well as by sea?" I exclaimed.

"Everything," he smiled.

This was now becoming ridiculous to me. To pull this off in a "den of thieves," which is what Iraq is, plus the Greeks on top of it all? Remember, Greece is where the Middle East begins. It certainly wasn't like mailing a parcel by UPS.

"John, I'm past my prime and out of the business for the most part, but if you can get assurances on the payments, I'll see what I can do to help you with a tanker. Hell, a little excitement wouldn't hurt me. Retirement gets a bit boring, you know? Besides, whatever happens in Liverpool," he concluded. "Don, did you ever hear of this little band called the Beatles?" All they did was change the world! I knew Don would help. He had always been loyal and supportive of my father.

I flew back to Iraq via Paris. I needed a couple of days to mull this over on my own. This particular June, Paris was very warm and more beautiful than ever. There truly is, despite any other claims, no city in the world to rival it. If it weren't for the French, it would be earthly perfection.

Farqad contacted me immediately upon my return. I had candy for his children, Chanel No.5 for Bessrad, French magazines for the girls and Cuban cigars for Farqad. It was a *Rive Gauche* care package for the already over privileged. I also bought Farqad's "man" a couple of bottles of expensive Scotch whiskey and candy for his children. The man cried. Farqad whisked me off to his study to learn what had developed. Did I have the numbers? I told him this was not a good place nor time to discuss this, but yes, I did have the information. But now it was time for food and merriment and I would meet him tomorrow in his office and to bring Mr. Al-Hashimi, our friend and lawyer with him. By the time I returned downstairs, much of the candy had been demolished and the girls were frolicking in the perfume.

It was growing dark on a warm, starlit night. Various members of the household were spread throughout it, most notably Farqad, who was fast asleep from food, booze and flab. There was a two-seat swing made of wood in the front of the villa. I went with Naji to sit on it, waiting for Farqad to wake up and drive me home.

"Naji," I said. "The next time you put on perfume, the idea is not to take a bath in it."

This was the closest I'd been to her since I met her and she was even more radiant in the soft moonlight.

"I know, Mr. John, but this is a real treat that has not happened in eight years ever since the Iraqi people were prohibited from travel. We were just having some fun, that's all," she said. Suddenly, she became very sullen.

"I will die here, unwed. There will be another war, a war of great consequences," she said.

"You don't know that for certain," I replied, trying to appear optimistic. Naji was a different woman; not wedded or living overseas or wild and promiscuous like her other sisters. A solo tear ran down her cheek. I wanted to hold her, to comfort her, but I dare not touch her where we were sitting, in full view of the house.

"Come with me," I said and led her around to the side of the house. We were out of view from all except a rustling in the bushes. I could hear giggles and knew who it was immediately. Akmed and Hassam, Farqad's sons, were hiding in the bushes.

"Come out of there," I whispered. They came out rather sheepishly; knowing anything they did with me was a risk.

"Here, now go away and say nothing," I said. I gave them each a ten-dollar bill. They were elated. I'm sure they already knew how to get seven dinars to the dollar from their classmates at school. I turned back to Naji. The scent of the perfume was mixing with the musk of her anticipation. Its aroma was intoxicating.

"Naji, I'm going to kiss you on the lips, hard, for a long time," I feebly uttered.

"I don't know what to do," she said timidly.

"I'm going to hold you by your hair and tilt your head to one side, softly. Just close your eyes and part your lips slightly," I said.

I touched her hair. It was thick and soft as silk. I could feel a stiffening in my pants already.

I slowly pulled her head toward mine and kissed her pouted, red lips; as sweet as cotton candy. It made my head spin. Suddenly, she threw her arms around me and I did likewise. Her ample bosom pressed against my chest and I could feel her erect nipples through my thin shirt. I thought I was going to come in my pants! Although it lasted only a minute, it felt as good as all eternity.

Coming to my senses, I backed away and she realized it was over. We walked around to the front of the house. Farqad had risen from his stupor and was now prepared to take the drive to my hotel. Naji turned to me and smiled. As I walked away she said softly, but audibly, "Thank you" and with that, we speed off into the darkness of the city.

Farqad was sweating bullets. Farqad always sweated, even if the air conditioning was on high. After what I began the conversation with, he was a veritable ocean.

"One billion barrels!" he exclaimed, his voice trembling and reaching for his ever present glass of water. It splashed out of the sides of his mouth and down his beard as he gulped. He kept wiping his head with his handkerchief. I sat there sipping Iraqi coffee with Hashimi, the lawyer. The coffee was brought to us in a perpetual flow by Farqad's office boy, a lanky, black Arab from the Sudan. Anwar Sadat's father was a black Arab.

"Well, Hashimi," Farqad asked. "Is it possible?"

"Possible, yes. Practical, no," Hashimi said. A straighter answer one could not ask for.

I liked Hashimi a lot. He received permission from Saddam to open the first, privately owned and controlled bank in Iraq in forty-five years. What made this easier was that the Saddam family had a piece of the action. Hashimi hired me as an independent consultant to help him build it. He was always taking me to lunches and banquets at what used to be a British country club, now just a garden restaurant for the Iraqi elite. He was always introducing me to powerful people in the country. Hashimi was very quiet but equally fearsome.

Farqad chimed in, "This would have to be planned down to the exact detail."

"There is no word in Arabic for planning," I said. Everything is *En es Allah*, or 'if it is Allah's will'. That loosely translates to good fucking luck!

Farqad went to a chalkboard, his office being in a pre-automated stage.

"How long to do it?" he asked.

"One calendar year, maybe less," I said.

He scribbled with the broken chalk while clutching that handkerchief so hard it was wringing itself out. Farqad was, fortunately a numbers man and needed no calculator.

"What field could pump at the level needed and still remain within OPEC restrictions plus that supply?" he said.

"Rumallah," Hashimi said.

Rumallah was an oil field in western Iraq. Geologists determined its size to be technically unfathomable, meaning limitless or certainly more than 100 years.

"The Kuwaitis' have encroached on the field mile by mile while we were off fighting the war with Iran. Now the lower two-thirds are in their control," Hashimi said. "We don't know exactly how much we have left."

Farqad ventured on, "What about force?"

"Perhaps one day, but not now," Hashimi cautioned.

To stop this ping-pong game, I broke in. "Let's assume for a minute it can be done. What's today's price per barrel of crude?"

"Roughly," Farqad said, "Twenty to twenty-two dollars a barrel."

"Even at twenty, that's roughly $2.2 billion gross," I said, not really being too sure about my math; it was not one of my better subjects.

The Iraqis' were beginning to tug at their collars.

"Commission, who knows about commission?" Farqad inquired.

"Based upon some rough estimates I obtained from our oil people, you're looking at one half of 1% per barrel which is .05 to the dollar," I said.

"Yeah, and multiply that times one billion barrels and tell me what you get?" I wanted to know. Farqad banged away at the board.

"That's almost fifteen million dollars!" Farqad screamed.

Hashimi lurched forward. Farqad dropped both the chalk and his jaw. I just asked for another cup of coffee.

There was a lot of research to be done. Don called from England to tell me tanker reinsurers had been found rather routinely. The overland journey from the fields to the loading facility was our problem however.

Farqad looked into the queue of ships waiting to be filled in Basra. There would be minimally fourteen ships on average ahead of us. It would take months to fill no doubt, if not longer. We were going to have to get help from inside Iraq to pull this off. Where to get the commission money physically to? That was my problem. Hashimi would act as counsel for a fee; that's all he wanted. He already had his bank but could be a government go-between if necessary. More problems than answers, but the process had to begin somewhere, so we started.

The Minister of Oil was one of the nine ruling members of the Revolutionary Command Council (RCC). He was an older man with a bitch of a wife who was rumored to have even more power and influence than the Minister himself. Farqad knew him from the "old days," but they were not close buddies. Farqad, as was his style, floated around the outskirts of the issue with the Minister, trying to feel him out. The Minister exclaimed as we all previously did, that this was a massive deal; however, a letter of credit for ten percent in dollars deposited in a Zürich account might get things going. Once he gained official government approval, that is. The commission would be couriered to Cyprus and deposited in a Barclay's branch. It would be safe worldwide.

If the whole thing blew or for that matter worked, Farqad and his family might have a chance of making it to Cyprus alive if they could reach the Jordanian border. Since the Saddam's were getting a piece of the action through Hashimi's bank, he was untouchable, particularly since all appeared to be quite legitimate from the surface.

But the queue and the piracy? These issues could not be quickly resolved. Regardless of this, I sent a message back to Dr. Knobel we had a "conceptual go" on our end and for him to start the wheels in motion.

Late one evening, Farqad called me at my hotel. I was preparing for bed. He said he needed to see me immediately. I moaned about the hour of the night, but I complied. His "man" would be there in twenty minutes to pick me up. It was a chilly night for Baghdad.

When I went up, only the coffee boy was there. It was too late at night for this potent brew, but I couldn't resist.

"You sent for me?" I began. Farqad was nervously sucking on a cigar, a bad one at that.

"Yes," he said. "I'm sorry for the late hour."

"There is more information you should know," and with that he dismissed the coffee boy.

"First off, I want to give you half of everything my accounting and tax practice earns. I will open an account for you to keep the money in and you can have this money anytime. Next year, five years, whatever, it will be there for you."

"It is not necessary," I said. "You earned it. I just made some timely introductions."

"No, no, I insist," he continued. "Without your help, none of this would have been possible."

"All right," I replied. I had no intention of letting him do this. I had a second cup of coffee.

"The ship queue and protection," he said.

"Yes, the great unsolved," I responded.

"I have found a way to bump us from fourteen to four," he informed me.

"That's terrific news," I exclaimed.

"No, not terrific, terrifying," he continued from within a cloud of smoke.

"I know the Minister of Oil's wife," he began. Now, I started chain smoking.

"I met her years ago and did some accounting work for her. She maintains other businesses, other relationships," he said rather sheepishly.

"All this was unbeknownst to anyone, including her husband. She wears the pants in the family, anyway," he continued.

"She has agreed to move our ship and subsequent loadings for two million dollars," he choked out.

"It could be worse," I said.

I had yet another cup of coffee.

Farqad continued, "I'm certain she went to Saddam and she is taking a separate cut so she now knows about the deal personally."

That was not good news.

"The 'protection' overland will be provided by two men, probably Revolutionary Guards, at a cost of another one million dollars," he said. I winced.

Farqad implied, "We're still walking away with a fortune!"

"If we walk away," I said uncomfortably. "Is there more?" I wanted to know.

"There is more," he said. "I will pay the bribes out of my share of the commission," he firmly asserted.

"Why, what's the catch?" I asked him. "Is it then an 'Iraqi' affair?"

"To a large extent," was his response. He continued, "You brought this deal in, what is left will be more than I can spend in my lifetime, my friend."

I sat there quivering, mainly from caffeine.

"I have one final request," he said, his head now down and grim.

"You now realize, but may not fully understand what we are involved in," Farqad stated rather coldly.

"If anything happens to me, get Bessrad, the boys, and my sisters-in-law out of Iraq anyway you can," he said, almost in tears.

"Bessrad would never leave if she knew you were alive," I stated with firm assertion.

"Drag her out," he replied.

"Naji is yours if you so desire, but she does not know I've consented yet and I want it kept this way for a time," he said.

I looked him in the eyes. "How could you have ever known?" I asked him.

He smiled a wide grin; reached in his pocket and pulled out two ten dollar bills and slapped them down on the glass table.

"The boys!" I exclaimed.

He looked at me, still smiling and simply said, "*Abu* (father) knows everything!" He broke into a huge Santa Claus laugh.

A thousand thoughts slammed through my head on the ride back to the hotel. I was speeding on caffeine and cigarettes. It was all so mind-boggling. I couldn't even think of Naji.

Upon returning to my room, I sat on the edge of the bed thinking. All my life, I wanted to be dangerous and suddenly I was! It wasn't as much fun as I thought it would be. I didn't even take my overcoat off. This oil business sure looked a lot easier when I saw it every week on *Dallas*. I was so wired that at 5:00 a.m. I was still awake.

In the weeks that followed, we all worked diligently to move our respective parts forward. The Greeks, as I anticipated, were giving us the most trouble and from the beginning, I couldn't help thinking Dr. Knobel was double dealing all of us. He just fit the profile.

I went to see Naji at another one of Farqad's infamous dinner parties. We were getting closer all the time. Everyone kept staring and smiling and giggling. The boy's however, had a sour look on their face; I'm sure still smarting from having their bottoms fanned for the last incident.

"They all know," Naji beamed.

"How?" I asked.

"Bessrad forced it out of Farqad. He had to tell her everything in case … well, you know, just in case," she answered.

"Are you happy?" I asked her.

She pierced me with those emerald eyes and said, "I would die for you."

Although brief, I stole one last kiss before I left. Seven million or Rita Haworth? Was it worth it? Which did I really want to happen more? I just didn't know.

Dr. Knobel couldn't control the Greeks. They were in, they were out, the Iraqis' were thieves, you name it, and there was no end to their suspicions. As I always tried to remember, Greece is separated from the Middle East only by a body of water!

The deal was faltering as pressure mounted from the various players in Baghdad. There were numerous inquiries from "higher places." As it did once before, the telephone in my room rang late at night.

"Farqad here, you must come to my office now," he said rapidly. This time I didn't make a fuss.

When I arrived, he was sitting at the end of the table looking worn, very dejected. I said nothing and took a chair.

"I believe it is in our best interest to back out of this deal entirely," he began. There were tears welling in his eyes.

"It is not like the Mafia here," he continued. "First, they kill your cousins, then your aunts and uncles," he said, trying to regain some composure.

"Then they systematically move on to your in-laws, sons, and daughters. They arrest your friends and associates. Then they kill your parents and torture your wife until she confesses to whatever they want until she dies," he said. "Only you are left alive to witness it all." I sat there in horror.

"I have a good life, a loving family and thanks to you, a growing business," he pressed on.

"True, I am not as wealthy as a prince, but I am content and a king in my own kingdom. I do not need this money to be happy, to be content," he confessed.

"And if this fails, what will they eventually do to you," I asked point blank.

"Hang me," he said passively.

"And me?" I gulped out.

"You will rot in an Iraqi prison until you die." What a comforting idea; I wasn't going to hang, just be eaten alive by rats!

Farqad asked me, "Is this worth the chance of failure, of a double cross, or any of the unknowns?"

"I'll call Knobel in the morning," was all I could get out. I rose from the chair and walked out into the alley, which even at this hour was alive with smells, and the laughter of life.

I found myself, once again, sitting on the end of my bed, overcoat still on and hands in my pockets. Seven million fucking dollars out the window, just for brokering a deal. And Naji, I could still taste her on my lips, like rose petals, her skin as golden as honey. All gone. Dreams and schemes. I phoned Dr. Knobel who blamed everything on us and the Iraqis.

"You could give the deal to Mark Rich, he's based in Zürich," I offered.

"Don't be ridiculous," he replied.

President Gerald Ford outlawed political assassinations in 1976. If the US government were to create a top ten list of people they wanted dead, Mark Rich would rank about sixth. Rich was notorious for bad oil deals, constantly unbalancing the global economy.

And what about my European job? Well, I knew that was bullshit from the beginning. I never heard from Dr. Knobel again. When later on in my career, I did go on to consult to a German electronics giant and got to live in Munich, I discovered the anticipation was not worth near the deliverable. And Farqad and I? Well, it was on to bigger and better things!

CHAPTER 4

Professor Backwards

I have a nickname for almost everyone I know. Dr. Tomasz was "Professor Backwards." Dr. Tomasz was a semi-retired, New York cardiologist who also owns a medical consulting company. I first met Dr. Tomasz in the Pan Am waiting room in the Frankfurt airport on our inaugural flight to Baghdad, where we had the opportunity to while away twelve hours waiting for the connecting flight. Over a leisurely breakfast of whiskey and pound cake, I remarked that the reason we were wasting the day in the waiting room was that Citibank was too cheap to spring for day rooms in the adjourning Sheraton hotel at $50 for an eight hour stay!

Everyone called Dr. Tomasz, Dr. Tomasz, even his wife. The good doctor is a likeable, somewhat eccentric American of Iraqi lineage. His past, not unlike his present, is somewhat dubious. As best as I could trace it, he was born in Baghdad, raised there until the age of seventeen and immigrated to the United States. On a boat ride to cross the Tigris River, simply to get to the other side, he said he had not been in one of these canoe-like crafts since he was a boy. He noted this while standing at the front of this sliver of a ship, with nine of us jammed in it, looking more appropriately dressed for a yachting regatta, in his double-breasted blue blazer and ascot. He claimed not to speak Arabic, but every time he was spoken Arabic to, he appeared to know exactly what they were talking about. How could anyone conduct business in Iraq for all those years as he had, let alone go in and out of Baghdad like it had a revolving door and not speak a lick of Arabic? I don't know and to this day still do not know!

It was through his contacts with the regime that Citicorp was awarded the contract to rebuild the Rasheed Bank. For this feat, he was to receive three percent of the gross billable for the total amount of the contract ad infitem, plus whatever I didn't know.

His consulting firm was primarily involved in arranging medical operations in the United States for wealthy Iraqis. You know, the type you see British waiters fawning over at tea at Claridge's, stuffing their face full of scones and cream, sitting there in their robes while you're turned away for not wearing a tie! He also imported pharmaceuticals into Iraq. An issue of *Vanity Fair* magazine published some years ago accused him of ripping off the Iraqis' to the tune of $40,000 on drugs that were never delivered. Dr. Tomasz vehemently denies this charge. He claims to hold hundreds of patents for medical equipment, equipment he supplied to the Iraqis as well as medicine and was never paid the equivalent of hundreds of thousands of dollars.

As my association with him matured, the experiences became even stranger. Dr. Tomasz was able to come and go into Iraq as he pleased, a privilege he still enjoys to this day. Even with the UN embargo still firmly in place, he performs, with full Senate approval and under the guise of humanitarian aid, to treat children who are burn victims of Desert Storm. In addition, he has flown planeloads of them to the US for treatment. Meetings with the Assistant Deputy Prime Minister, and the former Minister of Finance of Iraq were arranged with little effort, and yet with all that visibility and goodwill over the many years, he claims never to have met Saddam Hussein, nor until UN brokered meetings in New York, Tariq Aziz, although supposedly he knew him as a boy and was his de facto physician. He'd rather discuss once having had the opportunity to treat Elizabeth Taylor!

When the team first arrived in Baghdad, we were required, as are all foreign visitors, to have an AIDS test. This was mandatory under the penalty of a significant fine, payable only in US dollars (but of course) and imprisonment, for all those staying more than seven days. Imagine an ACLU field trip to Baghdad? You talk about civil rights!

To his credit, Saddam had limited the number of known AIDS cases in Iraq to two, both attributable to blood transfusions required for surgery in Europe. I, as did the others, envisioned the use of used needles, rusty razor blades as well as other nightmares of third-world medical practices. Dr. Tomasz stepped into the breach and informed us he would use his significant influence to have us excluded from the unpleasant ritual. As test time drew closer, our threats of non-compliance grew more grandiose and Dr. Tomasz continued to reassure us we would not be subjected to the test. The night before our scheduled "invitation to infection," several of us chained ourselves to the Rasheed Hotel bar, vowing to remain there all night in such a stupor that they would be unable to perform the test. One actually stayed the distance until the morning.

The Doc remained steadfast to his position. As the morning of our reckoning arrived, we assembled in the hotel lobby at our usual departure time for the bank assured us we had beaten the Grim Reaper and were free of the test. I confidently walked up to Dr. Tomasz for the official confirmation and when I asked if it were true, that the bank said no test, he launched into a diatribe, incomprehensible to the average mind, intricate as needlepoint and fantastic in its proportions. As I began to grow increasingly nervous, the story continued to the point of the Doctor taking great personal delight in his oration. Finally, exasperated, I screamed out, "Doc, do we or do we not have to have the fucking AIDS test?" He ceased his tale, looked me straight in the eyes and simply responded, "Yes." Hence, Professor Backwards was born.

We hauled Jack out of the closed bar where he was passed out, kicking and screaming, and all went off to the hospital. What ensued was shocking. The hospital was sparkling clean. The test was of the most modern variety, which could also diagnose gonorrhea. Steve immediately remarked, "Hey, wait a minute. Nobody said anything about gonorrhea!" He had just come to Baghdad via Bangkok. The nurse was so incredibly gentle I could not even feel the needle go in. After its removal, she cut the tip, put it in a separate bag and sealed it.

I felt like a ninny. I asked her if the test results were negative, would she like to have dinner with me. She did not find me very humorous.

At that point little did I realize that before my stay in Baghdad had ended I would become an expert in third world medicine. After we had not been in Baghdad very long, my dear friend, Hikmut, took my colleague Pat, and myself on a motor tour of the city and out to lunch. My first inclination something was asunder was when I did not see the name of the restaurant in the Michelin Guide book. We referred to these joints in the States as "Tomain Tommy's!" I ordered what I believed was the safest dish in the house, chicken kebab, some rice and veggies. Pat scarfed his down, but then Pat would eat shit regardless of its place of origin. If I knew Hikmut as well then as I did later I would have said, "Are you out of your fucking mind taking us to a place like this?" But being polite, I ate it and said nothing. The restaurant was across the street from the race track, and I wondered what they raced there (horses, in Dubai, its camels) and if this was a buffet of the losers.

Within a few hours, my asshole dropped out. I figured, "Okay, got rid of that and what have we learned from this picture?" But it didn't stop; it went on and on. By day three, with Lomotil (cement for the asshole) failing, I was growing weak and dehydrated. I finally cornered Dr. Tomasz, informed him of my malady and he replied, "I'll fix you up with some pills later on." That evening, Steve observed my skin had turned a lovely shade of gray. Doc showed up at the bar with capsules he said were antibiotics strong enough to knock out gonorrhea. Wonderful! Now I didn't have to worry about my dick falling off. They didn't work. He suggested I see a doctor. I said, "I thought that's what you are!"

He said, "No, a local doctor who can do a stool evaluation, culture, etc." and off to bed he went. Doc once told me he only needed two to four hours of sleep a night, but for a guy in that robust health, he was always off to bed early. I would have suspected him of getting a little on the side, but since I had already asked him where the local whorehouse was and he didn't know (or so he said), I dismissed it. He gave me the name of a local witchdoctor who spoke English. Dr. Korkis was so old he had treated Farqad when he was a boy and

Farqad was ten years older than me at the time! Nonetheless, he was a kindly old man whose hands shook terribly. Meanwhile, I was still shitting!

By now we had been temporarily moved to the Baghdad Novotel Hotel. It would remind one of a permanent Quonset hut. It was October and time for the annual Baghdad Trade Exhibition. Every year at this time, Saddam takes over all the hotel rooms in the city for three weeks and disperses them to foreign companies and dignitaries participating in the fair, or more appropriately, another of his foreign currency capture schemes since everyone must pay in dollars, deutsche marks, francs, etc. No funny money. Even the damn Vietnamese showed up. Upon our arrival, we were informed there was no hot water, but that it would be available in about forty-five minutes. This went on for three days. Same question, same answer. Baghdad is still quite warm in October, but this is not the way I like to start my day, particularly with a night's worth of shit matted to your behind! The front desk manager was the type of guy you'd like to toss to a bunch of Hells Angels, just for the sport of it. By morning of day four, I was in the lobby to register an unrelated complaint when an angel of mercy appeared in the form of a sergeant from the UN troops stationed there. He was bigger than "Too Tall Jones," the NFL player. He asked the proverbial same question about the hot water and was given by now the standard answer, "In about forty-five minutes." The Sarge reached over the counter, pulled the desk clerk over the top of it by the neck and screamed, "If there isn't hot water in forty-five minutes, I'm going to use you for a scrub brush!" It must have been by the grace of Allah, but in about that time there was hot water. Not to be outdone, when the manager gave away a reserved room for one of my staff at in the middle of the night, I threatened to call the "Big Man" himself, Saddam, right then and there (I was only bluffing). Low and behold, another miracle, instant room plus champagne!

Dr. Korkis came to the Novotel and started me on some pills. He took no specimen. No success. Different pills, different colors, same results. This went on for three more weeks with no change. Dr. Korkis' hands shook worse. Pills in different amounts, pills in different combinations. My weight dropped and starting at 123 pounds, I didn't have much to spare. Ribs began making their appearance. The "LA look."

"I know what you need—energy. Something to pep you up while we wait for this to pass," he remarked on one nightly round.

Enter liquid Vitamin B12, straight from the bottle, legal "speed." Within a couple of days, my skin began to reek like an old Rexall drug store; the kind with the wood floors that absorb every aroma. The smell reminded me of when I was in England and they used to feed the chickens anchovy-based meal and when you took off the cellophane, the chicken smelled just like fish. Now why did I endure over a month of this you may wonder? Stupidity comes to mind, but that's too rational an answer. Working for the true humanitarians I did, I was afraid if I went to London or Frankfurt for treatment, my firm would replace me with another Project Manager and at that time, I was desperate to stay employed.

John, the Citibank chief, phoned from his warm, safe haven in New York one evening and asked me what I was doing. I replied, "I'm waiting for Dr. Korkis."

He responded, "You're kidding?" I replied what reason would I have to kid him about something like this and asked if he wanted to speak to the doctor himself, like I was a kid caught lying. He passed.

By now, some internal muscle or other body part would occasionally protrude itself from the vicinity below my ribs. My quick wit deduced, that now, for real, I was truly in deep shit!

The old man arrived with yet another elixir of some type and, you guessed it, more pills! Yeah, just what I wanted!

I told him in the immortal words of Roberto Duran, "no mas, no mas!" He shook worse. He insisted I take them. I threw him out.

I was beginning to worry how I was going to go on. Since I had trimmed down to ninety pounds, I became the topic of constant conversation at the bank.

"Where was Dr. Tomasz and why wasn't he attending to this problem?" the bank officials wanted to know.

"He isn't in Iraq," I answered.

Sylva, my secretary, had a brother-in-law who was a doctor. He studied medicine in Ireland (good one, huh?). He was affiliated with the very private Irish Hospital in Baghdad. This is a hospital that treats two classes of patients, wealthy or connected to the regime. The hospital was not open to foreigners unless they had a letter from their country ambassador. April Glaspie, our ambassador, as was the norm, was unavailable.

There are armed guards in every corroder to repulse the unwanted or to stop you from getting any Irish pussy. Yes, as far as foreign talent, this was the only show in town. Every pisshead who ever touched the Blarney Stone tried to score here. Sylva's brother-in-law gave me the name of an Irish doctor whom he had approached about my problem and who said he would help me, but not at the hospital. I called "Dr. James" one evening at the Rasheed Hotel and arranged to see him there one evening. Jim was one of the nicest, un-God like doctors I've ever had the pleasure to be sick in front of. He was aghast at my physical state and asked what I had been doing to myself. After a brief explanation, he produced a small vial and a tongue depressor and told me to go take a shit in the bathroom and scoop off a bit into the vial. You know, about as much as they give you on a little spoon when you ask for a sample at Baskin-Robbins ice cream. Then I was to tell him when I was ready and he'd package it for transportation. I thought, "What an unpretentious guy; he's going to get his hands in shit right here in his hotel room!" He gave me a preliminary list of dos and don'ts and told me to return in two days.

"Parasites, two types, probably from unwashed vegetables," he announced. Game, set and match! Within twenty-four hours of his medicine I felt better, two more days more so, and in four days I was well on the road to recovery.

I went back to Jim to give him another "flavor of the month" sampling on the little spoon. After a few weeks, they were completely gone. During the last visit, Dr. Jim and I had a chat. It seems he was one of the founding fathers of the Irish hospital some six years ago. Now, he only visited a few times a year for a couple of weeks at a time. He asked me about Dr. Korkis and all the drugs he gave me. After

I recited the Physician's Desktop Reference to him, he enlightened me with a few details on the practice of Iraqi medicine. According to Dr. Jim, Dr. Korkis knew his medicine wasn't working, hence so many combinations of different drugs. The poor old goat had to find something to knock the bug out of my system. As time wore on, he became more desperate.

"Why didn't he just tell me to go to the West and get treatment?" I asked him.

"Because he was under instructions from the Minister of Finance to cure you," he replied. The Minister of Finance was my indirect boss in Iraq and the project sponsor.

Jim continued, "And the Minister's boss is Saddam, so you get the picture?"

I'm afraid I didn't, but then it was early days there and I hadn't read any chapters from Saddam's "Book of Horrors."

"If his medicine didn't cure you, they'd send him on a one-way holiday!" Jim replied.

I said, "You're joking?"

Jim didn't answer.

Now I understood why the old fella's hands were shaking so much. I said nothing more. I guess it didn't really register. It seemed too big to believe at the time. No one is ever that important to cause another one's death. I decided it was time to stop sleeping in pajamas with the feet on and wake the fuck up! I tried to pay Dr. Jim but you've got to be kidding me. I never saw nor heard from him again. Ditto for Dr. Korkis, but for different reasons.

When Dr. Tomasz saw me in New York at Christmas time, he was horrified at my resemblance to a poster boy for Biafra. This was my first of many Dr. Tomasz's "after the fact" reactions that continued right up until his convenient disappearance from Baghdad shortly before the Kuwait invasion. Dr. Tomasz and I were ardent enemies throughout the project, doing battle over minor, usually cost-related issues. Now, I love him like a father.

I managed to displace his cousin as the bank's general counsel with a man loyal to me. Score one for me! Dr. Tomasz managed to get a Citibank financed fax machine, difficult to obtain permission for in Iraq and enshrined it in his local Baghdad office, about an hour by car in local traffic from the bank. Score one for the Doc. I insisted on having Farqad as the bank's accountant over Dr. Tomasz's handpicked choice. Score another for me.

Two to one for our side! And so it went, on and on. But he trumped me one when he arranged for the bank's executives to visit Citibank in New York and fly by private jet to visit a software vendor in Orlando and visit Disney World. The Chairman of the bank returned with Mickey Mouse watches for his grandchildren and Doc gloated. As he waxed nostalgically over the trip, while rubbing it in, he related a story to me of their stay at a local hotel.

"It was a warm, moonlit evening," he began. "The breeze was blowing ever so gently and swaying the palm trees." You have to imagine Doc telling me this in his blazer, ascot, and pipe. "The stars reflected the tranquility of the evening." Majid Al-Ani (the bank Chairman) and I strolled hand-in-hand (as is Arab custom among men) around the hotel parking lot, discussing world events.

I burst out laughing! He asked me what was so funny about an obviously personal matter.

I said, "You probably looked like two old queens." He was not amused.

Ed, our former Managing Partner and I had lunch in Washington, DC, after Desert Storm was successfully completed. Ed was a very paranoid type. I guess you have to be to survive as long as he did in the consulting game. He bugged his office, as well as his briefcase, with a kit he purchased from a "spy store" on K Street. Ed had been considering doing some business with Dr. Tomasz for his new start-up venture.

"Have you read the recent book on General Norman Schwartzkopf, the one where he makes all these unflattering remarks about Saudi defense capabilities?" he asked me.

No, I had not but I had read some of the highlights of it.

"There is another part of the book that elaborates on the uncanny ability and ease with which US airpower was able to conduct bombing raids with almost pinpoint accuracy," he went on, becoming very animated.

"You mean the 'smart bomb' technology?" I replied.

"Yes, exactly that," he said while panning the restaurant to see who was coming and going.

"Like the bomb we dropped on the building where they thought Saddam was hiding and wiped out 409 women and children in Al-Amiriya?" I asked him.

He sat there expressionless.

"And the baby food factory we bombed that we thought housed some kind of bio-tech manufacturing?" I continued.

"And the bomb they called the 'Saddamizer' or the 'bunker buster' or whatever the fuck name they called the thing?" I pressed. It was time to let Ed off the ropes. "What is your point?" I asked him.

Ed looked at me with this wry little smile and carried forth regardless.

"The book states that this type of strategic bombing would not have been possible without high-level, very detailed intelligence, more than just satellites could provide. Information that had to come from within Baghdad," he explained.

"There were spies everywhere, so what?" I pointed out.

"To procure this reconnaissance, a person would have to have virtually unrestricted movement in and out of Baghdad, a person almost above the law with the complete trust of the Iraqi authorities," he said.

By now, Ed was almost in a lather and the Crab Shack resembled an EF Hutton commercial, with everyone straining to hear this conversation.

He continued, "Someone who could go in and out of Baghdad like it had a revolving door!" A sickening little pattern was starting to develop.

"The book implies that the information given to the Allies came from someone with at least access to Saddam's inner circle, but it's conceivable that whoever it was could have been a double agent." I thought all this bugging stuff was affecting Ed's mind.

Since Ed never considered another person's welfare, I knew he had some self-serving interest in all this from the line of questioning.

You could cut the tension in the air with a knife. This was the political center of the world.

"I've been considering a professional association with Dr. Tomasz on some business in the Middle East and, uh, I was wondering, uh, I mean. I'm obviously pumping you for information, I hope you don't mind?" Ed said.

Not exactly knowing how to respond or what I wanted from this encounter, I simply stated I would have stopped him if I took offense. As is true with most consultants, he more than likely overstated his ambitions, oversold himself and already had forged this alliance with the good doctor.

"Get to the point, Ed," for I was anxious not to be late for tea with a friend.

"Do you think that Dr. Tomasz could be that agent and if he is, whose side do you think he's really on, ours or theirs?" he asked me.

People in the restaurant were now craning their necks in anticipation of the answer.

My only response was a smile and a deep laugh inside my soul. Professor Backwards a spy, let alone a double agent? I wonder, I really wonder!

To this day, Dr. Tomasz's humanitarian aid to the Iraqis' continues. He has become the unofficial "babysitter" of whatever level Iraqi delegation comes to complain to the U.N. to lift the embargo. He methodically maintains a position of neutrality on this and other issues and will carry on endlessly about the suffering of the Iraqi children if coaxed. I guess it's good that someone cares about the endless misery they, as a people are enduring. No one else in Washington seems to. Doc has to care; if he stops his only chance of recouping the enormous amount of cash Saddam owes him and the US government won't let him have will be about as successful as their invasion of Kuwait!

CHAPTER 5

The Spy Who Went Out in the Cold

Remember Wally Cox, the original *Mr. Peepers*? He was the nerdy-looking humorist with the narrow chin and round wire frame glasses who sat underneath Paul Lynde, America's funniest fairy, on the Hollywood Squares television show. A real *Casper Milquetoast*-type of guy. Well "Dr. Smith" was a cherubic version of that character. One spring evening, I strolled into the restaurant at the Ishtar Sheraton Hotel to find Steve and other colleagues dining and chatting with a man I did not recognize.

"John!" Steve shouted over the din in the room. "Come over here. I want to introduce you to someone you should know," he said.

As I was usually in a foul mood at the prospect of another excursion into nausea, I replied, "Why?" By this time, Steve was used to my mood swings and just ignored them. I can't say I could blame him, for at times like this I could be quite rude, obnoxious and generally had great difficulty just being with myself.

"Dr. Smith, this is our project manager at the Rasheed Bank, John Norman," Steve began. "John, Russell is the commercial attaché at the United States Embassy here in Baghdad," Steve said.

He shook my hand with a rather clammy, effeminate handshake. My first impression of Russell was that he was gay. He was reserved, yet pleasant, neatly attired in sport clothes with sandy gray hair, a bit portly, somewhere in his very early fifties. A career diplomat, he was an intellectual, a historian at that (an

Egyptologist), but clearly not a snob. Probably at the worst, a professional type, a typical PhD who was just to the left of genius, but a lousy businessman.

We exchanged business cards and pleasantries, promising to call each other and get together for a meal. It was the type of arrangement you make with someone in California but never have any intention of keeping, you know, "let's do lunch!"

Everyone at the table, particularly Steve and Lee, a want-to-be diplomat and intellectual, seemed particularly anxious for Russell and me to spend some time together. I couldn't really fathom why. I never had any prior experience with the Central Intelligence Agency, let alone how they operated in the field. Usually, the CIA bureau chief was a high-ranking diplomat of a most unassuming nature. Russell Smith fit that description to a T!

A month or so passed before we again made contact. We were about to enter a session of "can you top this," or more commonly, who could ask each other for the most outrageous favor. Russell initiated the game by asking me for a brief report on the exact nature of the work we were performing at the bank for a monthly briefing to the State Department. After clearing the request with New York and Washington, I told Russell I would do it, but required more detail as to the content he wanted. I dispatched Lee to the US Embassy to speak further with Russell about the subject. Lee showed up ready to go in exactly the attire I expected to see him in; blue blazer, crisp white shirt, preppie tie, gray slacks, and penny loafers. It was enough to make me gag! I instructed him that under no circumstances was he to attempt to talk with April Glaspie, the US Ambassador to Iraq, nor was he to make any quotable statement about the project at the bank. Clearly disappointed at my distrust and this lost opportunity at stardom, he reluctantly trudged off on his rounds.

Russell was most appreciative and suggested we have dinner and I accepted on the condition I could drag along Farqad. Russell agreed and suggested I also bring along Christy, another of my erstwhile employees and the only female of the group. It was my first indication that Russell preferred the company of females, let alone young, available ones. I figured, *what the hell give the old fart a thrill!* and said

I would extend an invitation to her. Although Christy was a bit of a ditz, at least she was good to look at.

Farqad was a wreck and there's not much worse than a fat person when they are nervous. He wasn't sure what to say, what not to say, proper decorum, whether the restaurant would be appropriate and a litany of other mindless detail.

"Relax," I told him at a warm-up meeting. "You'll do just fine. Have a couple of blasts at home beforehand to calm down and follow my lead. Be yourself. You're a regular laugh riot!"

It didn't work. I could understand why. For years he had toiled in this fourth world stinkhole to build a humble, localized tax and accountancy business. Now he was coming face-to-face with the might of US capitalism at a time when Saddam had capitulated to foreign business interests for the first time in eight years, due to the war with Iran. This was the fat man's shot and he was going after any and all commercial relationships that Russell could generate and I could make materialize.

The evening turned out to be a veritable bonanza for Farqad. We dined in a quasi-continental restaurant in the Al-Mansor Melia Hotel, a five-star monolith across the street from the state-controlled television studios. Christy cleaned up nicely and looked splendid. Russell ogled and drooled. The desired emotional response had been achieved. Farqad had belted a few whiskeys as prescribed by me and was poised, agreeable, and generally entertaining. Russell, as it turned out, was having a difficult time negotiating contracts with the Iraqi authorities for the likes of General Motors and Johnson Controls, amongst others, and could use all the help he could get in structuring these deals and interpreting the complex local tax laws. Farqad was only too happy to accommodate him. Russell offered to recommend the use of Farqad's various services as a local representative of credibility to the senior executives of the firm's as well as putting him on a type of retainer for other generalized counsel as required. Farqad was beaming and I was delighted for him. It was his time in the sun.

The check came and Farqad grabbed it, as I knew he would. As is Arab fashion, he never displayed his money, but he peeled off several large notes from his wad under the table. We walked outside into the warm moonlight and bid Russell farewell. He was in no pain either.

Farqad yanked me near out of my shoes in a great bear hug. His size and strength was scary when he had been drinking. I had gotten accustomed to being kissed by Arab men, more a business necessity and cultural requirement that enjoyment, except Farqad could be quite sloppy about it when he was drunk. I finally slipped his grip and suggested we get Christy back to the hotel before she passed out, as she was not much of a drinker. Besides, it might be my golden opportunity to jump her bones! (I didn't).

Johnson David was an employee of the bank assigned to the modernization effort, consigned to me by the accounting department. Johnson was basically a likeable enough guy with the exception of one irritating quality. He was usually drunk, day after day for most of the day. I was afraid to smoke around him because he always stunk of whiskey and I was afraid we'd blow up! Most of the men in the bank detested him and the women were afraid of him.

Once I needed a driver to take me to the US Embassy and Johnson volunteered. A short time later, I found out why. On the ride through the city, I asked him, "Johnson, you have a relatively decent job, a car, a house, and a family. Why do you drink so much every day?"

He glanced over at me with a glazed expression, that empty stare of hopelessness I'd come to recognize on so many Iraqis' and said, "Mr. John, look around you. This is all we have. It will never get any better and there is no way out."

He may have been a drunk, but he was not stupid, for after the amount of time I had been in Baghdad, I could understand what he was feeling. For someone of his sensitivity and intelligence, it was a viable alternative, for he had accepted his fate and given up.

Russell surprised me with an invitation to dinner at his villa. He lived alone in a modest house not far from my hotel with his Filipino housekeeper. His wife had not yet joined him as she was teaching in Washington and waiting until the end of the school year to finish. As it turned out, he was also waiting for his furniture and personal affects, so the house was sparsely furnished. He introduced me to his maid after a brief tour of his house and we settled into his living room with a couple of drinks to wait for dinner.

Russell was more relaxed and charming than usual. I was genuinely beginning to like him and enjoy his company. Like me, he could be caustic and cynical. I also was growing unfortunately intoxicated with the power, prestige and control my relationship with him was providing me, not only with my own people and the Iraqis', but also within the international diplomatic community and US and Arab corporations. He spoke for the first time about April Glaspie, for I had yet to meet her and from what I had heard about her, I did not want to.

"April?" he replied, settling into a paunchy position at the end of the sofa.

"You mean the Queen?" rolling his eyes with an obvious look of disdain. "The Queen" was the nickname the US Embassy staff had bestowed upon her and it just about summed it up. A truly "royal bitch" in every sense of the word!

April Glaspie was a scholar, a historian of the Middle East, raised by her career-diplomat parents in Egypt. She was fluent in several dialects of Arabic. She was apparently a good information gatherer and pulse-taker, the primary job of an ambassador in a post such as this; a loyal tail-wagger who dutifully reported all she observed to the omnipotent Secretary of State, James Baker. April had only met three times personally with Saddam Hussein during her tenure. In the last meeting, she accompanied the US Undersecretary of State for Mid-East Affairs and was relegated to a chair behind the men and definitely out of camera range. This was an indication of Saddam's opinion of her capabilities. Why the State Department would delegate a woman to such a sensitive, crucial diplomatic role in any country in the Middle East, let alone Iraq, is beyond my analytical ability.

Women, for the most part, have the equivalent status of cattle throughout the Middle East. Iraq was forced to liberalize its treatment of women out of necessity, not choice. During the war with Iran, women came out of the household to become the business infrastructure of the country while their husbands and sons were being slaughtered at the front. They became used to new freedoms, such as earning money, wearing Western dress, nylons, lipstick, etc. At the completion of the war, they were reluctant to give up these new found perks. As it turned out, a generation of men were lost in battle and of those that did return, many were maimed, crippled or amputees and therefore unable to work. The men did not relish the female phenomena, but were forced to accept it.

The majority of the workforce of the bank was women. I found them eager and competent, the men lazy and bitter. The men initially treated the sole female on my staff, Christy, with similar contempt, albeit with a certain politeness since we were foreigners. However, the men remained professionally uncommunicative, making the documentation of specific business requirements difficult for Christy to complete and the end quality product poor.

Further complicating the matter was the century's old trauma of losing face, not just to a man, but to a woman. The way to ensure that they did not appear to know less than her about their business, therefore, preventing the possibility of this happening, was willful non-compliance. The men did not understand the role of a consultant. The term was anathema to them, regardless of gender. Having no prior experience with this, I only realized the mistake I had made in recruiting Christy for the job well into the project. It was only through force, the only thing an Arab understands and respects from a motivational standpoint, with the backing of the bank's Chairman, that I was able to surmount this problem. Still, throughout the project, they remained cool at best toward her.

Being less than a devout Muslim and a fancier of women, Saddam was more lenient than any of his Arab counterparts in the treatment and attitude to women. This most definitely made my tenure there a more visually appealing experience, but you still couldn't get any pussy!

It is not difficult to understand, bearing in mind these facts and the dictator's contempt toward her, why April was incompetent in dissecting Iraqi internal affairs, and unable to foresee the Iraqi invasion of Kuwait. This single event cost her position of ambassador, for which she was cruelly chastised and unfairly and unmercifully banished from the diplomatic corps. It was the failure of the State

Department in assigning a woman to the position in the first place, not in April's inability to carry out the mission. Any old Middle East "scholar" or old hand, whom the State Department has an overabundant surplus of, could have told Jim Baker that!

There was a clamor in the kitchen and we shuffled in to see how the meal was progressing. Russell's maid was in the process of trying to prepare a spaghetti dinner, complete with homemade Italian sausages (Yes, real beef from a butcher in Baghdad). But she hadn't quite gotten the hang of it.

"The sauce needs herbs," I said. "Do you have any oregano and basil?" I inquired. She motioned toward the cupboard.

"You can cook?" Russell exclaimed in amazement.

"My grandfather was from Naples," I said. "Hand me that ladle, will you?" I motioned. The fact of the matter was that I was a gourmet cook and not just limited to Italian cuisine. I cook primarily as a form of relaxation. Tasting the sauce, I told the maid it was too bland and dumped in a glass of red wine as well as an assortment of herbs into the pot.

"Well, now that I know this, the next time you can come over and cook the meal from scratch," Russell declared.

I said he had a deal. As it turned out, the meal was passable, better than average. When you are living in a hotel for long periods of time and eating every meal in a restaurant, a home cooked meal is a welcome diversion, even if the food isn't any good and that wasn't entirely the case here.

"John, I need a favor," Russell said prior to settling in for brandy and coffee. It was his version of handing me the check!

"In your capacity as project manager in the Rasheed Bank and your access to the Chairman and other key figures, I assume it is possible for you to audit restricted information on specific financial transactions?"

"The Chairman has nothing to do with it, but for argument's sake, let's say it is possible," I answered poker faced as I could muster; for it was obvious he was speaking from a State Department standpoint.

"Okay, fine. Is it then possible to manipulate data within accounts, let's say so as to hasten a particular payment one customer owes to another through the bank routinely processing that account?" he pressed on, his anticipation growing.

"Sure, Russell, many situations are feasible depending on the risk you want to take, but for Christ's sake, look where the fuck we're sitting! The penalties and repercussions could be quite severe if anything appeared remotely out of order," I continued. "Is this a matter of national security?"

He then sat back in the sofa. I assumed he had already discovered what he wanted to know.

"No," he began. "It is not. It is a corporate affair of sorts," he said.

Well, I thought. Now he's going cryptic on me.

"It involves a much delayed payment of funds from the Iraqi government to a US business concern and I, uh, just thought well, maybe you could assist on expediting the matter," he said, now appearing rather sheepish.

Luckily for him, I didn't know enough yet to be scared.

"Russell," I said. "You're going to have to trust me enough to give me the details."

He grinned. I was reamed, steamed and dry cleaned!

"All in good time, my boy," he said. "All in good time."

Johnson David pleaded, "My wife, Mr. John, she has relatives in Chicago. We'll only stay two weeks. I promise on the life of my son, I swear to you."

I truly hated these moments, for I have never suffered from a God complex. For the first time in eight years, Saddam Hussein had relaxed the restriction preventing all Iraqis from traveling out of the country. This of course was contingent upon procuring the relevant visa to the destination of your choice. Every head of family or individual traveler was allowed exit with only the equivalent of $700 dollars in whatever country you chose. This, therefore, severely restricted what you could do and where you could do it. How long could one last in New York or London with $700 at today's prices? Not too damn long, that's for sure! The Iraqi dinar, according to

American Express, was worth the equivalent of ten American cents. In other words, it was as useful as toilet paper. So if you did not have relatives abroad to look after you, you didn't go.

I told Johnson I would make some inquires, but I knew I was bullshitting him. Besides, all I had to do was do this for one person and I would be besieged with requests from all of them.

Russell telephoned rather urgently with the information I needed to check the account in question, as I knew he would. It seemed relatively straightforward enough, but in all honesty, I didn't even know where to begin to look, or more importantly, whom I could trust to do the looking. I decided to ask Hikmut, an Iraqi scholar of Kurdish descent, who was assisting me with the bank's strategic planning and had become a trusted friend. He in turn told me he would help, but it was more complicated than I thought. It required someone in the accounting department to tell us the status of the account, the process the bank followed to do the wire transfer and someone in the Central Bank to dispatch the transfer.

"Jesus," I said. "The authorities?"

"It is the only way," Hikmut answered.

I decided to go over to see Russell at the embassy. I had a plan.

"A visa for the information, are you serious?" Russell shrieked behind the closed door of his office.

"Look, it' the only way I can find out the payment scheme," I implored. After all, it was no skin off my ass, for I wasn't getting anything out of this deal and Russell, for whatever motive he really had, wanted this done worse than before.

"Will this guy come back, I mean, can we trust him?" Russell wanted some assurance. The embassy was not in the immigration business, particularly for Iraqis!

"There is no guarantee, but everything he owns is here, his house, his bank accounts, job, and pension. They still do mean something in Iraq, even if they don't mean shit in the States. I have to have an inside man and this guy is it or you're shit out of luck!" I said with some finality.

"Deal, John, do it," he reluctantly replied.

"Johnson, do you give me your word that you'll come back? Because if you don't, I'm fucked, and the US Feds will hunt you down like a dog," I pleaded. Even as I said it I knew it was useless.

"Oh, Mr. John, you have no worries with me. All I have is here, how could I stay in America, how would I work?" he said in an alcoholic haze.

"All right, here's the deal, you get me the status of this account and find out the process for overseas payment in as much detail as possible and you and your family get visas to the States. You can present the results personally to Dr. Smith, understand?"

"And Johnson," I continued. "No one is to know anything about this. If someone in the bank asks you why you want to know this information, make up some bullshit excuse. When it comes time to travel, tell anyone who asks that you got the visa on you own accord, even though they'll figure it out in time, got it?" I explained.

Johnson was a nervous wreck on the way to the embassy, but at least he was sober, well almost. It was terrible to witness a person in such a grip of fear over what you and I would consider to be routine. After the usual security check, I wheeled Johnson in to see Russell. We exchanged cordialities and Russell, anxious to get on with it, wasted no time.

"Whaddya got for me Johnson?" he said, taking a brief second to try to read my expression. Johnson was now sweating profusely and the faint odor of whiskey began to fill the air, circulated by the ceiling fan.

"Dr. Smith, this is a complicated process that I will do my best to explain. All the foreign companies owed money by our government are ranked and paid first, by the amount of time the government has owed the money and then by the amount of the debt, broken down by certain cut-off points," Johnson explained. Russell looked confused, as I had expected.

"So what does that mean and how does it work in all practicality?" he asked Johnson.

"Let's take an example," Johnson suggested, standing up for greater dramatic effect. I was just hoping he didn't fall over the desk!

"Say your company has been owed money for two years," he began. "Those invoices would be paid first because they have been due the longest. Then within that two-year period past due, we would pay, let's say bills in the range of $150, 000 to $200,000. When all of those have been paid, we would then move to a spread of $100,000 to $150,000 but still two years past due, until all the outstanding items were paid off down to zero for the two-year past due period. Then we would move to one-year past due at again set amounts, then six months and so on and so forth until, en es Allah, someday, all accounts past due would be current and satisfied."

Johnson then produced some back dated records to serve as an illustration of what he meant. To translate it loosely, the Iraqis paid you when they damn well pleased, unless you were marked as a priority. This usually only pertained to defense contractors. That is why the backlog was so huge.

Johnson sat back down, apparently pleased with himself. At least that made one of us. Russell looked puzzled, but with good reason, for he still didn't have a clue about how to resolve his dilemma. I urged Johnson to continue.

"The firm you have inquired about is only owed some $35,000 dollars and is delinquent only three months," Johnson said.

"Based on the formula I have just explained the firm in question actually falls into the second lowest to be paid for the year, the lowest category being $15,000 dollars or less."

"Yeah, yeah, so what does that mean?'" Russell pressed.

"It means with the current backlog, they can expect payment in well over a year from now," Johnson concluded.

Russell, for the first time in my experience with him, threw a shit fit. "A year? A year! That just won't do!"

"It is our way," Johnson said, looking down apologetically.

Russell knew the poor man had done what was required of him and adjusted himself to show a more appropriate decorum.

"Thank you, Johnson," he said. "This information, though disheartening, is quite useful. Did you bring the required documentation for your visas?" he asked. Johnson beamed, opened a manila envelope and handed over his passports, visa applications and pictures.

"These will be ready in about two weeks. I will contact Mr. Norman and he will collect them and give them to you. You've been most helpful and you have my thanks. Now, could I privately have a word with Mr. Norman," he demanded.

Johnson almost shook Russell's arm out of its socket as a Marine escorted him into the anteroom.

"Oh, great," Russell said in his most despondent tone of voice. "Now what?"

I said I didn't know, but I'd think on it awhile and maybe something would come to me. I started to back out the door and Russell grabbed me by the arm.

"Will he come back, John?" he asked.

"Russell, I'm certain of it," I said.

"Yeah, right," he replied, rolling his eyes and disappearing behind a mountain of paper.

Mayada Lateef Jaffir Khaydim was beautiful in the classic, Arab tradition. With black hair the color of ink, cherry red lips and porcelain skin, she was the kind of beautiful that made men stupid. She was a college graduate and a telecommunications engineer at the bank. I was gaga over her and she knew it. Once, upon my return from Switzerland, I promised myself I wasn't going to be so obvious and go running into her office, so I didn't see her for two days. When I finally ran into her in a hallway, she looked at me with her dark cow eyes and pouted lips with a wry little smile and said, "I knew you were back, why didn't you come to see me?" She knew she had nailed me good. One of the things I loved most about her was her caustic, acidic wit. The more she twisted the blade in me, the deeper I sunk! We had many interesting conversations, several of a most intimate nature, for she was most curious about sexual relationships between American couples. There is always something more erotic about discussing sex with a woman who is not only beautiful, but has a body to die for! On one such occasion, she equated premarital sex with buying a pair of shoes. When you know you like the style and color and you know your size so they will fit without question, why must you try them on? Well, back to the drawing board!

I knew it could never be in my wildest dreams for it was culturally impossible. Never, ever, would a Muslim woman be able to wed a Christian man, particularly since most, if not all marriages, were prearranged or brokered. An affair would bring disgrace to the family and could cost the woman her life. So my hand and I dreamed on. What a pity! In a land where the women were beautiful, curious, and numerous, where it was virtually impossible to contract AIDS, you couldn't touch a one of them!

Once, while looking at Mayada from a distance, I said to my colleague Tom, our company lounge lizard and communications guru, "Do you realize that no man has ever seen her pussy?"

Tom looked at me with a smile, salivating from his gold-filled teeth and said, "I don't even think she's seen her pussy!"

Mayada often had a look of sadness of her face that I could never quite figure out. There were marriage prospects, arranged by her father, but there were none she would consider because she wanted to love a man. I asked her what her relationship was like with her father and she described him to be more like a manager than a father, although she said she knew he loved her. But she believed that no one could ever be capable of loving her the way she wanted and needed to be loved. If she only knew.

Russell again summoned me to the US Embassy. He looked terrible and despondent.

"I've just gotten my ass reamed by Senator Pell," he wasted no time in beginning. I guess that now he was really ready to talk.

"He wants his money and he wants it now!" he said with his forehead resting in his palm.

"What's this all about?" I demanded.

"The company I had you look into is owned by Senator Pell and his Iraqi partner. The company manufactures military insignia and sold a large consignment to the Iraqi army," he explained.

I was somewhat startled, but not shocked.

"A US senator selling to the enemy so to speak?" I asked Russell, who looked relieved at having this out of the closet.

"There's no law against it, John, at least at the moment," Russell protested.

JOHN NORMAN

I did not know much about Senator Pell, but what I did know I didn't like. A paltry sum of money as the amount in question was peanuts to a man of his family's wealth and heritage. I was suspicious that this deal was just the tip of the iceberg and that this entrée into the Iraqi military machine was part of a larger, munition related relationship.

Russell continued, "This is just the first payment in a series of many, what the total due will be I'm not certain of." Okay, it wasn't the end of the world. He now adopted a more somber tone.

"He called me personally to threaten me. It could be the end of my career if I don't resolve this soon."

Marvelous, I thought. What's a little extortion amongst friends?

One morning in late June, Mayada came to my office alone, which was unusual. I always relished the pistols at ten paces conversations I had with her.

"What's on your mind?" I asked her. She smiled, and I expected honey to begin to ooze from her lips.

"I would like to visit America in the summer. I have a cousin who lives in Tennessee who has agreed to look after me," she said.

"Great," I exclaimed. "I will be in North Carolina all of August. Maybe we could see each other?"

"Perhaps, but I have one problem and that is why I need you to help me," she pleaded. I wondered what could be so wrong.

"The Americans will not grant a travel visa under any circumstances to single Iraqi women. They are afraid Iraqi women will entrap American men into marrying them so they can get residency. I have heard it is easier to go through Canada and then to the States. But I know no one who could help me to get a Canadian visa either. Is there anything you could do to help me?"

By now, I was like Jello. Short of marrying her, which I might have considered, it appeared hopeless on the surface.

"Let me think about it," was about all I could get out. Then in an instant, I had one of the wildest ideas of my life!

"Are you out of your mind?" Russell screamed. "That's not a deal, that's putting a gun to my head!"

74

I knew him by now. After the initial reaction, his logic banks switched on and rationality regained control.

"Here's how it works, Russell," I began. I was truly energized by how dangerous this was and the prospect of getting into Mayada's pants (yes, a stiff dick knows no conscience!)

"All the women in the accounting department love Hikmut and most of them are Kurds, his people, so they naturally hate the Iraqis and will do almost anything to fuck them up. Besides, he'll bribe only one of them to look the other way. Then he'll take the physical invoice and move it up in position near the top of the heap. When she discovers it's out of sequence, Hikmut will explain the oversight, tell her to leave it be and explain that it would be best if she just processes it and stays quiet about it. If necessary, Hikmut will say it's for Mr. John and if she ever wants a visa out of Iraq that maybe I could arrange it. He knows someone in the Central Bank who owes him a serious favor. That woman will make the transfer to Pell's account in the States and bang-o! It's over. No one is the wiser and you're off the hook! It might cost a few dollars here and there but at this level, it will be nominal. What do you think?"

"And Hikmut's willing to do this for me?" he asked.

"Not for you Russell, for me, for the future," I replied.

"John, Mayada is single. Washington will have a hemorrhage. Wait, I have an idea! Is it possible for you to write a letter on your corporate stationery stating that Mayada works directly for you and she is going to the States to take a course for her work for you? It should also state that the course is for a limited time only, is offered nowhere else at this time but in the States and you will accept full responsibility for her return to Iraq."

Without waiting for an answer, he added, "And John, your boss needs to sign it!"

He had a Cheshire cat grin on his face.

"No worries," I said. I'll forge his signature I thought to myself.

A week later, Hikmut informed me the transaction was completed successfully and nobody was even remotely suspicious. All it cost was Hikmut having to take the woman in the bank that did the switch for us to dinner and he was pissed at me, for of all the beautiful women in the bank, she was the only real bowzer!

I arranged to meet Mayada at ten o'clock in the morning in a restaurant two blocks from the US Embassy. I told her to look her best and as I watched her get out of the taxi and walk towards me, she had definitely outdone herself. Mayada looked nervous and concerned, but then I expected her to. She spoke hurriedly and her English fragmented.

"I must speak to you before we go in to see Dr. Smith," she said. Mayada was looking down at the ground. I lifted her chin up with my hand. It was the first time I had ever touched her.

"I cannot go to America," she began. "My father has tricked me!" She remained composed. It was me that was about to come unglued.

"You see, he had contacted my cousin in Tennessee and had arranged for me to marry him shortly after my arrival there. My auntie, who is my best friend, could not stand to see this happen to me, so last evening she told me the truth and I confronted my family."

"What did they say to you?" I asked.

"My father tried to deny it," she said. "He told me my cousin was a good match and this marriage was acceptable to both families. He said I was getting old and soon I would become undesirable to any man."

I found this to be both unbelievable and believable all at the same time.

"And with your temper you managed to control yourself?" I asked.

"Yes, he is still my father. I told him I did not love my cousin and would not do this awful thing. I will marry only if I ever find love. The women defended me to him. He gave up and called my cousin to tell him."

I was saddened for her, yet relieved that she was strong enough to fight her fate.

"Well, this is, among many other things, lousy timing," I said. "We might as well go in and tell Russell, since we have an appointment anyway. Who knows, there may be a chance to go later in the year and it won't hurt to have met him just in case I'm not here," I explained. Mayada wanted to know what reason I would give Russell for her canceling her plans.

"I'll tell him the bank cannot spare you right now, that we are at a critical stage in the project and you must remain in Baghdad to participate in it."

We walked down the street and into the embassy compound. The scene was total chaos. There were hundreds of Iraqis lined up waiting to get in for visas with Marine guards policing them. We strode past them and I whipped out my passport and held it aloft. They ushered us past the yelling crowd and into the security zone. I must admit that the power to do something like this felt great. I knew there was little or no chance for most of these people to get out of this prison they called home.

We went into Russell's office and sat down. After the introductions, I explained the circumstances to him. I did not care whether he believed me or not, for he was off the hook for his part of the deal. Russell just sat there, a drooling old fool, trying to sneak a gander between Mayada's legs. I can't say I blamed him!

On the way back to the bank in the taxi, I asked Mayada if I could give her a small gift, something perhaps to remember me by. I had an ounce of Chanel No.5 I had bought in Paris in my jacket pocket. She said it was appropriate to accept a gift only if it was something like a pen. My mother enjoyed the perfume.

Mayada and her buddy Samira, came to see me during my period of captivity shortly following the Kuwait invasion; while I was being held at the hotel. She wanted to return a technical document I had loaned her. I was shocked and delighted to see her. I wanted desperately to pull her aside and talk to her, to tell her my feelings about her, for although this situation appeared hopeless, I did not want her to give up on me. My colleagues surrounded us and I couldn't get a word in edgewise.

Their visit was brief and I resigned myself to walking them to the front door of the lobby, which was as far as I was permitted to go. We stood there staring at each other. If you could find a way to paint pain, this canvas of us would have lasted forever. All we could manage was, "Goodbye." Mayada flipped down her Foster Grants and went out into the bright sunshine with Samira. I knew that I would never see her again.

April Glaspie went on her annual vacation three weeks before the Kuwait invasion of Kuwait. Dr. Russell Smith went away on vacation abruptly, certainly without phoning me, two weeks before the invasion of Kuwait. Coincidence?

Maybe!

CHAPTER 6

Colonel Strangelove

Prior to leaving for another trip to Zürich to review the progress on the Focus methodology (how to assess a country's economic and natural resources regardless of location), or my quarterly sanity check, I had a rather unusual request from Farqad.

"On your way back from Zürich, I want you to stop in Nicosia and see Colonel Bob," he requested, looking more round and jovial than usual.

"And whatever for and who will bear the cost?" I inquired in mild sincerity.

"Oh, I'll explain it all later," he said, as we were at the bar in the Sheraton Hotel and like most public places, he feared it was bugged and there were secret police everywhere.

As chance often has it, I never had the opportunity to speak to him before my departure and before I realized I went from the baby-shit brown of Baghdad to the rich, alpine green of Switzerland. As always, I was glad to return to the land of the living, in a city with people I had grown quite attached to. As was now my norm, I camped out in the Hotel Eden-Au-Lac, not a stone's throw from downtown Zürich and near our local office. By all standards, the business of review, discussion and amendment was quite boring but very necessary as we had already received payment for the Focus process and had never adapted its use in the Middle East before. But I never really cared about how mundane it all was, for it was an opportunity for boutique shopping, call girls, poached turbot, MTV, and cavorting with my Swiss colleagues.

In the middle of an overstuffed, relaxing and utterly non-eventful week, I received a phone call from Farqad in Baghdad. Farqad wanted to know if I had made the booking to go to Cyprus.

"Made the booking," I remarked. "Made the booking?"

I still had no idea where I was going, why I was going and who Colonel Bob was.

"Are we on a secured line?" Farqad asked.

"You're the one sitting in Baghdad and you're asking me that question!" I said.

"You are right," he answered. "Here is the telephone number in Nicosia. Call him and introduce yourself. He knows who you are and what this is about. Tell the bank you could not get a direct flight back to Baghdad and have to spend two nights waiting for one in Cyprus. If you think that will create a problem, pay for it out of your own pocket. It is very important to me that you go there. Do it for me John, my brother," and the line went dead. I guess his nickel was up! How I hated that "brother" shit. It always went right through me, especially from Farqad. But for whatever the reason, I knew it was critical to him and I called the Colonel to set it up, and then scheduled a flight to Larnaca.

As it was winter, I arrived in the dark although it was still early evening. Customs was a breeze with the natives friendly with pleas to stay long so you can spend more of your US dollars. I was quite surprised upon exiting the terminal that all the taxicabs were Mercedes-Benzs.

"Hmmm, no one starving here," I said to my otherwise uninterested driver.

"Welcome to Nicosia, the largest listening post in the world!" No, the sign at the city limits did not say that but it just as well could have. This was the "Big Party," every fucking spy in the world and his or her brother was in this place. Nicosia served as a communications and coordination center; the consummate staging area for terrorists of every nation and race; Turks, Greeks, Arabs, Reds, you name it. All broadcasting from Iran and Libya was monitored here. Lots of banks, translators, mercenaries, the infamous import-export companies and last but not least, weapons dealers. A veritable "take-out for terrorists" and right in the middle of it all, the smooth as silk, deceptively deadly, cigar smoking Colonel Bob!

I had made a reservation at the local Hilton Hotel. The Nicosia Hilton, like most American-owned hotels in large Arab cities, served as the social gathering hub and cultural center, a place for Arabs to see and be seen, and as this was a Friday night, it was more decked out than usual. Men in cheap shiny suits, gaudy watches, patent leather loafers, and drenched in noxious cologne abounded. Not to be outdone, the women were in various designs of pastel colored, 1950s cocktail gowns, porno star pumps, two inches of pancake make-up, cheap jewelry, big hair, and mandatory beauty mark. Have I covered everything? They also reeked of "Oh de Toilet." Everyone smoked. An insect didn't stand a chance in the place! Though they were not widely in use yet, whoever now has the local cellular phone franchise is today a billionaire. Mont Blanc pens had also yet to make it as the "pen of the privileged." My room, to no surprise, was not yet ready, so I reached for my suitcase, which was in the middle of the lobby, intending to haul it around with me.

"Leave it where it is," the clerk instructed. "This is Cyprus, no one steals anything here!" Yeah, right.

I asked for messages and there was one from the Colonel stating he was in the gym and for me to wait in the lounge. In the meantime, they'd made up my room, so I went up and unpacked, certain Bob was still getting buff. When I returned to the lounge, seated next to the only gym bag in the room (it's against Arab custom not to be fat) was the Colonel in the flesh. He looked like everything you would expect a Colonel in the US Air Force to look like. Tall and of rakish proportion, every hair in its place and fighter-jock handsome. I wondered if it was a good time to tell him I was once questioned by the FBI in Boston in the early 70s for a bungled bank robbery by the Weather Men Underground, an anti-war anti-government extremist movement.

He stood up and up, introduced himself and told me it was time to leave; that he had made plans for dinner but we had to stop and pick up his wife first. Margo, Mrs. F-14, was beautifully dressed in a plaid, Scottish type wrap-around thing and was as good looking as Bob. They hoped I liked Arab food (ugh!) and off we went to some nearby emporium.

Bob and Margo had been living in Cyprus with two of their three sons for the past six years. Bob was retired, but still on reserve status duty meaning that in the event of crisis, he would be called up in a minute's notice. I knew he had an intelligence background, but never directly confronted him about it. His business on Cyprus, surprise, surprise—import-export!

During his stint in the military and following his retirement from active duty, he had been a consultant to General Dynamics. Most of his time was spent in southern California, wheeling and dealing in airplanes for a variety of clients and purposes. He had become involved with a zillionaire Iranian and became something of his personal assistant, confident, goodwill ambassador, etc. He had come to Cyprus to set up the import-export company, concentrating primarily on steel. However, on Monday, he took me to his office in a bank. I said, "I thought you were in steel, construction and that sort?"

He looked at me beaming and said, "I am also a Director of this bank. Iranian money, you know, you can't keep it there anymore!" gesturing with his arm in the general direction of Iran. "He's already lost twenty million that is unrecoupable."

The day following my arrival, a Sunday, they invited me on a picnic with some friends and business associates of theirs. I awoke tired and worn; the Sunday stay in bed with the *New York Times*, tired. The weather was also dreary, for winter in Cyprus was no guarantee of sunny, mild skies. They appeared promptly at 9:30 a.m. and off we went to round up the guests. We met Bob's colleague in the import-export business, Eduard and his wife, in-laws, and kids. Shortly after, the party increased with a Russian translator and his wife plus a set of their friends. Everyone embraced rather warmly for this was a well-acquainted social set. We piled the chairs, blankets, picnic baskets and hampers in and headed for the hills outside Nicosia. In route, Bob explained some of the history of this controversial island from Makarios to Nikos Sampson, to the 1973 war (most of it brought to your living room live courtesy of the BBC) to the "Green Line," to the precarious peace that exists today. It seems the Turks got the better deal from the war; all the lush grazing land, orchards, and resorts of the North and the Greeks were left with shit in the South. I suspect when we're done with the Yugoslav civil war, the Second Korean War and Castro dying, someone will attempt to resolve this division, although I believe it will culminate in the much long awaited sequel, another Greek-Turkish War!

It is important to the average tourist's education that "Greece is separated from the Middle East only by a body of water" and "Greece is where the Middle East begins," complete with its corruption, reverse sense of morality, and the same complaints about everything, including our "do nothing" attitude about the Near and Middle East. It's why they hate us so but can't exist without us.

As we rambled through the rolling hills and villages with roads only wide enough for one car, it was visually apparent that the island was quiet as I expected, very quaint, and picturesque. We arrived at the planned picnic site about an hour later. The caravan pulled off the main road and down a dirt lane into an almond orchard. The farmer did not take very hospitably to this intrusion and had to be persuaded with as is usual in the Middle East, a few dollars. We unpacked the cars, set out the chairs and blankets and almost immediately, everyone started drinking. Although as charming as this all is I was miserable. As early as it was, I was ready for sunset. While Bob was trying to organize some outdoor activities, the Gods took pity on my plight. The temperature began to drop, the cloud cover intensified followed by a misting of the surrounding hills. The wind picked up, the kids began to cry and the Colonel called the games off on account of rain! We hurriedly packed up the autos and began the caravan back to town.

"Well," Bob remarked. "It was my original intention to just have this affair in the confines of a nice, warm taverna so John could soak up some of the local culture," he admonished while trying to navigate with a cigar clenched between his teeth and a can of beer in his crotch.

"Since this picnic was your idea in the first place, why the hell did you make us all go out in this weather when you must have known it was going to pour?" Margo exclaimed somewhat perturbed as she knowingly assumed the whole entourage was going to wind up at her house.

Bob just chuckled an "Oh well," and then laughed rather uproariously at what was an obvious reference to stupidity on his part by his wife!

One could never get angry with the colonel. He had an infectious sense of humor, extraordinary in fact, considering a man of his position and discipline.

We spent the entire afternoon having "picnic under glass" at Bob and Margo's comfortably appointed house, feasting on cold chicken dipped in garlic sauce and playing cards. Toward the end of the afternoon, Bob, Eduard and the Russian translator engaged me in a spirited round of global affairs. They began drinking the local version of Mextaxa, the Greek brandy, at increasingly regular intervals as the discussion became more controversial in its matters. They began politely to ask one another, regardless of the fact that Bob was their host, if they would like another drink.

"Well, if you're having one then I'll have one," was always the response. Then they would all toast some worthy cause or alliance, like gays in the military.

After three hours of this, I'd had my fill of cigarettes and diplomacy and asked for a taxi to my hotel, as all of them were by now rather drunk. Much to my disappointment, Bob insisted on chauffeuring me, laughing hilariously all the way to the Hilton while I watched for oncoming vehicles from every direction possible.

The following morning, we met in Bob's office. "Klinker!" remarked Bob, rather animated.

"Klinker?" I said. "What the fuck are you talking about?" I remarked the only 'klinker' I knew of was an off-key note or an unresonant fart.

"Okay, so I'm ignorant" I said. "What is it?"

"Klinker is a natural, small round stone or pebble of sorts that is essential to the production of cement," he explained. "The klinker can be exported here to Cyprus, processed with other ingredients and then exported to Pakistan for a massive road construction project. They require some four hundred tons. We'll make a bundle!" he exclaimed.

"The best klinker to be found is in Iraq," he continued.

"Seems quite straight forward enough, but since it required me coming here for such an elementary discussion, what's the catch?" I asked.

"The problem is it requires support from one of the ministries, most likely Trade and Finance, so Farqad and his contacts in the government will have to convince the Ministry that this is a good deal for Saddam," came the logic and the reason.

The word *convince* in the Middle East according to Webster's means "to bribe." As this was not a foreign term to me by now, it came as no great surprise.

I said all I could do was to discuss with Farqad whether this was an appropriate and profitable use of his human resource.

"Bob, you and Farqad, what's the relationship?" as this, the most obvious question from the beginning, was somehow overlooked. Eduard, who for the most part remained rather silent, gave me a conspicuous kind of glance.

"My father was the Pan Am station chief in Baghdad in the 1950s. Farqad's father was the former Undersecretary of State for Iraq. We are both Christians and went to Jesuit high school together. I haven't seen him but once since then, but we stay in touch. Now more so than ever," he explained.

It was a reverential explanation at least. So that was it, the reason behind all the secrecy and paranoia from Farqad. Just how risky was this?

"Mild, by comparison," Bob said. "It's straight forward supply and demand." I was less than convinced.

We adjourned the meeting for lunch. We were joined by a young colleague of Bob's from his bank who wanted to pump me for information on software development for banking applications. I didn't mind. It was a good diversion from the last two day's discussions.

As I began my discourse, Bob explained that as the host, it was customary and an honor for him to mix the group salad. While I talked, he sat merrily mixing oil, vinegar, and assorted spices in a wooden bowl, oblivious to the fact that he was flinging it all over his shirt and tie. No reason to ruin the ambiance of the day by telling him, I thought. We had a delightful meal of octopus in ink, the infamous salad, and lamb in yogurt and fortified Turkish coffee. On the way out, the colonel introduced me to the former mayor of Nicosia and also the local head of my company's competition. As is always the case with these partners, he began a rectal probe for information as to what I was doing in Cyprus, as if he owned it.

"Good for your business," Bob hastened to say as I was trying to back out of the restaurant.

"The devil takes many forms," I smiled.

It was then off to visit Kikos, Bob's accountant and erstwhile business advisor. "Beware of Greeks bearing gifts" is what his business card should have read! Bob told me now that I was going to be filthy rich; I needed a place to stash my money from the IRS and coincidently, where was the best place to do this?

"Why Cyprus, of course!" beamed Kikos.

They all, rotating the chair, went on to explain that there was no point in giving away my impending fortune. The approach, Kikos elaborated, was elementary business.

"You name three officers," he began. "One a President, one the Treasurer, one the Secretary. You are the President and make the Secretary your wife."

When I told him I didn't have a wife, as is also a Middle East custom, he offered his services to arrange a selection from which I could choose one or more if I preferred. I passed. He volunteered the Colonel instead as Secretary.

"You shall designate me as the Treasurer," he instructed, somewhat taken back at my lack of response to his gesture of goodwill.

"This is because I am an accountant as well as looking after the administration of your company here on Cyprus!" he continued. I can assure you this was less than a comfortable strategy but the Colonel egged him on.

"All the Cypriot government requires is a meager start-up fee. Our maintenance charge is about $2,500 dollars. You must also employ a local as, shall we say, a secretary of sort as an investment in the local labor market. You can pay her shit!" A real equal opportunity employer, Cypriot style!

"We'll keep the money in a foreign-owned bank, like Barclays," he said. "Then in case there's a coup or a war, we can access the money from any Barclays branch in the world. It's left to you to decide how much you want to tell your own government you earn."

"Oh, one other point. We'll keep Farqad's share as well in Cyprus. It will serve him better than in Iraq." Now there's sound planning if I ever heard it!

"So, what's the hitch?" I asked rather innocently.

"What do you mean?" Kikos looked at me disapprovingly.

"This is perfectly legal, right?" I said. "I mean with the Cypriots." They all nodded in approval.

"Then why isn't everyone sheltering money this way? It's better than stealing," I pressed.

Kikos, now taking on a new dimension in seriousness and pride stated there are currently over ten thousand foreign companies registered in Cyprus.

"Do you have $2,500 to initiate the registration?" he asked.

"Jesus, I just happened to have forgotten my checkbook at home," I said.

The Cypriots looked at each other quizzically, sort of in response as to why I wasn't elated at the prospect of beating my government out of my hard earned money.

Gratefully, Bob intervened. He explained that we should probably progress with the cement deal before we got involved with exchanging any funds; besides, we needed Farqad's commitment and approval.

I was relieved to say the least. Cheating the government is a major step in a man's development, certainly meriting further contemplation.

The hour was growing late and it was time to bolt for the airport and the plane ride back to Baghdad. Bob offered to drive me to Larnaca, a gesture I deeply appreciated.

It was a beautiful afternoon for a ride for the day had been pleasantly warm and sunny and we could look forward to a brilliant sunset, one of the few things about the Middle East I did enjoy. Along the route, he pointed out new housing developments clustering the hills. It looked more like a suburb of Los Angeles than a war-ravaged island.

We talked about the places we'd both traveled to and the conversation gravitated to customs inspections. He related a funny story, or so I thought, to me.

"There was a manager I knew at General Dynamics in Los Angeles," he began. "It seems that this guy had the job of going to Uganda to collect payment on a locomotive that General Dynamics had previously delivered. After an exhaustive $8,500 business class flight to Kampala, he found himself on a rather extended line in customs in the airport. He had been separated from other travelers by a leery-looking customs official. He kept trying to peer his way around the guy in front of him, but could not see anything. Finally, he asked this guy whose back he had been staring at what this line was for, since others, principally black Africans, were breezing right through. You mean you don't know? No, replied the manager, very innocently. You'll see, the guy replied. As they neared the entrance to a little anteroom, the manager stood agape in horror, unable to believe what he saw. There inside stood a huge, black official, rubber glove on one hand, just removing his finger from giving another traveler a rectal examination. In full view of others in the room, the poor bastard who'd just been done was wincing and trying to collect himself.

"You're joking," I said.

"No, and that's not the end," Bob said, trying hard to contain his laughter.

"The customs guy looked straight ahead, same glove on his hand, dripping with shit and said, 'Next!'"

I burst a gut. I damn near pissed myself I laughed so hard. When I could calm down a few kilometers later, Bob continued.

"The General Dynamics manager was in such shock, he left the line, found a government official, informed him he had a change in plans and began his odyssey back to California in total fear over the cost of the plane ticket, not coming back with the money and how he was going to explain this to the CEO!"

"Did he get fired?" I asked.

"No," Bob said. "The CEO couldn't understand what his man would have been so scared about. It was a perfectly good reason to hightail it."

"And this was before AIDS," I said.

"You got it," Bob replied.

"I guess I'll never really understand the psychology of what governs people in business decisions," I waxed reflectively.

Bob smiled and said, "If you do, write a book!"

He accompanied me into the terminal, and purchased some jellied candies for me to take back to Farqad's wife and kids. We made tentative arrangements to vacation together in Cyprus in the month of August; me, my folks, Farqad and his family, and in-laws. It was best to take advantage of the easing of travel restrictions out of Iraq while Saddam was still in a good mood. Bob would handle all the details for housing, cars, cash, etc.

We exchanged goodbyes and he departed. The visit had at least left me in good humor.

The deal never came off. In a follow-up phone call, Bob proposed our share was to be three percent, which Farqad and I would spilt. When I reacted in dismay, Bob explained that he was only making five percent and we would have to pool the funds for bribes to officials. Farqad and I discussed the arrangement and concluded this wasn't worth the hassle for a paltry payday.

It seems the klinker pit was quiet inland. Trucks often never arrived at their destination, in this case, the port of Basra. Farqad and I were responsible for the shipment arriving intact and for the cost of it if it did not. Farqad said it was better not to waste the time, the contacts and the bribe money on such a meager reward. I knew from the expression on his usually jovial face that he was hurt and saddened that as old and dear of a friend as the Colonel was more than likely, ripping him off. I cared for Farqad so it hurt me too. I knew fully what the pain was like.

As Desert Shield was shifting into full drama and high gear, I received a telephone call from the Colonel at my parent's home in North Carolina. After the initial pleasantries, he told me he was on his way to DC from Orlando by car and wanted to see me. Also, it would be a cheap place to spend the night. After my escape from Iraq and all the fervor surrounding the impending war, how could I refuse the temptation?

I arranged to meet Bob off the highway at a prescribed hour, since finding my folks place in the middle of the woods on dirt roads was impossible for "city people." He showed up two hours late in a white 1965 Corvette, a familiar cigar between his teeth with his uniform stashed in the trunk.

I poured a couple of drinks and my father initiated an interrogation that would go on through cocktails, dinner, and dessert. Actually, it ended at 2:30 in the morning. Bob was quite generous with what I considered to be otherwise highly sensitive information. He had been re-activated shortly after the invasion of Kuwait on August 2nd. Most of his time was being divided between two Air Force bases, a sub base in Florida, and the capital. He was now going back to DC to work on the logistics of the ground attack.

"Is there a plan to invade Baghdad by ground?" my father asked.

"Yes, most definitely," the Colonel replied, acting more like a colonel than I'd ever seen him.

"Is there a plan to kill Saddam?" my father, now in vodka overdrive, pushed.

Bob replied deadpan, "Yes, there is."

"Can you tell us anything about it?" Dad, now clearly pressing his luck, carried on. But what the fuck, it was his booze they were drinking and this is the price you pay for a freebie.

"It involves going into Baghdad and physically nailing him. That's what I'm going to Washington to work out now," was Bob's reply.

"Are you part of the team?" we all offered in unison.

A very flat, "Yes," he said and asked for another drink.

Later, in a more private moment on the porch for a late-night smoke, he elaborated a bit more on his view of the operation.

"Frankly, I'd just as soon be on the first tank in, do the deed, pull up in front of Farqad's house, take him to the palace and install him as the interim President," he said. Now his intentions per his old friend became crystallized for me.

I could just envision Colonel Bob riding atop a big star-spangled missile, whooping his war cry, saber and pistol in hand, slamming right into Saddam's palace!

"Thank God you took matters into your own hands and got out of Iraq on your own," he continued. Without grilling him any further or offering a number of alternatives as to what could have happened to me if I didn't, I simply asked him why.

He looked at me with a crooked smile and said, "Because I wasn't quite sure at the time how I was going to get in there to get you out!" I said it was nice to be loved.

The following morning, out he paraded in his full uniform, plastic government issued shoes, *Top Gun* glasses, silver eagles shining off his lapels, hopped into his 'Vette and went flying out in a cloud of dust, off to see the Wizard.

Sometime after the conclusion of Desert Storm, Bob returned to North Carolina again, this time on a very different mission. Mercifully, my parents were out of the country at the time, so it was possible to be more focused than his previous visit. We decided to hold this round of discussions in a local eatery. I had a friend in college who was trying to decide upon a career path and knew I had connections in the spy biz. I figured it was a good time to turn him onto to Colonel Bob.

"You didn't tell him I was an operative, did you?" he inquired on the way out to the video store where my friend worked.

"No, not exactly," I responded lying. I didn't want to lose my stream of free videos! When we arrived at the shop, my friend just stood there, mouth open, staring at Bob, resplendent in a crusty old bomber jacket, starched jeans and cowboy boots. Bob fired off a barrage of exploratory questions. The poor kid was speechless. To salvage what I could, I told Bob that I would act as a sponsor for my friend when the time came and whisked the Colonel out the door, leaving my young friend to deal with a line of irate customers kept waiting outside while this dialogue ensued.

"I want you to consider coming to work for me, on a special project," Bob began.

I asked if it was legal or covert. "Legal, oh yeah, of course," Bob said. "But we want to keep it low-key at the start."

The Colonel went on to describe an elaborate, delicate plan to rebuild Iraq. Saddam had put down the Muslim Shiite rebellion in the south and the Kurdish revolt in Erbil in the north. He had yet to nail the Kurds totally nor had the United Nations yet imposed the no-fly zones. Bob, through military, diplomatic and business channels, had coerced financial commitments from several nations to reconstruct Iraq, regardless of the fact that Saddam remained more firmly than ever in power. Even Iran and Saudi Arabia agreed to contribute to the fund and the amounts dedicated for this were already in the billions. The Japanese were reluctant and wanted a United States guarantee of twelve billion dollars before giving the four billion they were targeted for.

"You're serious, I know, but how would the American people react after all the emphasis placed on the recent war?" I asked.

Bob said, "I expect once they see pictures of the carnage, destruction, maimed, people and starving children, they will view it more as an act of mercy toward suffering mankind and cave-in."

"And how do you intend to distribute this wealth and where do I fit in, since fund raising is not my forte?" I asked him.

He had proposed that a bank be chartered and located in Zürich. This bank would act as a repository for the funds and would oversee their disbursement for Allied-approved reconstruction projects explicitly. No monies were to enter the regime's hands directly. Relief agencies and outside contractors would handle the construction projects and humanitarian aid. It was anticipated that this effort would require two years to complete and at its conclusion, the bank would be disbanded. It would be staffed with an international community of world-renowned bankers, negotiators and diplomats. I was to act as Chief Information Officer, or head of all computer technology.

The salary and expenses were a generous offer so I took him more seriously than my conscience was telling me to. Besides, it was Zürich, not some third world stinkhole as was usually my luck.

"What's the probability of succeeding in convincing Washington, for I assume that's what you're going up there to do?" I asked.

By now we were up to dessert and Bob was contemplatively sucking on a cigar.

"Pretty good, I think. I have some princely sums identified and a solid level of foreign support. So Jim Baker should be sympathetic," he said.

"Baker?" I said.

"The one and only," he replied. "There's a chance I might talk to the President as well. Want to go?" he asked quite determinedly.

People began to drop their forks and buzz rather excitedly even though the restaurant, a yuppie watering hole, was quite noisy and we made an effort to talk quietly.

"No," I said. "I think I'd be a bit outranked in that conversation. Besides, I have to watch the farm while the folks are away," I added, not feeling the least bit disappointed.

We left rather abruptly (I got stuck with the check again, even with all these billions!) and I asked if he'd be stopping on the rebound. He would not as he had to return to Florida.

Some time passed before I risked a call to find out if I needed to get my sweaters out of camphor. Bob had been recalled again, but I finally tracked him down to a Holiday Inn near the submarine base where he was working.

"Well, how'd it go with Baker and Bush?" I began after exchanging some strained pleasantries.

"Didn't see the President, too busy," he said.

"And Jim Baker?" I asked. "How receptive was he?"

"He threw me out!" Bob said and hung up the phone.

The Colonel returned to civilian work with some remote attachment to his Iranian colleagues. He telephoned me a year or so later and wanted to know if I could broker a deal for eleven, slightly used Gulf Air commercial planes. He told me it was the commission of a lifetime; that I'd never have to work again! Now where did I here that line before? I could use his offshore company as a front.

"Bob, go back to writing foreign intrigue novels, you'll be happier!" I recommended.

He just laughed his Colonel's laugh and said since he couldn't get anyone to publish his two prior books, that he'd have to stay in the trench coat business a while longer!

Old spies never die they just fade away!

94

CHAPTER 7

We Gotta Get Out of this Place!

August 2, 1990, had been a day I had long waited for, but not for any of the reasons that very unexpectedly happened on that occasion. This date was my scheduled departure date for my annual vacation. Pat and I had reservations later in the evening on a Swiss Air flight to Zürich where we were going for a couple of days to check the progress of our Swiss colleagues who were working on the Focus methodology; which we had previously sold to the Rasheed Bank. Then it was on to Washington, DC, for a meeting with our boss and then I was heading for the pristine beaches of North Carolina for a vacation with my family. It was a rest that was most deserved and very needed, for I was burned out from this project. The plan was for me to go home for the month of August and return in September and "tend the goats," for this was the last scheduled month of the contract and all the project deliverables had been met. The contract expired on October 9th and then it was back to the States until January of the following year, while the Iraqis and Kindle Software, the Irish supplier of the recommended banking solution, dickered over the license fee of their product. This left plenty of time to arrange a contract with the bank for consultant services. Unbeknownst to our firm, Citicorp had offered Pat and I the second year of the engagement if we would break with our firm. John P., the Citicorp chief, had grown very distrustful of our boss. There had been serious words concerning the quality of a credit card project at Emlak Banksi in Istanbul. John did not call our boss a liar, but rather eloquently stated that he had a "difficult time telling the truth." John did not feel comfortable doing a second year with our firm in charge and since Citicorp owned the contract, they could do with it as they well pleased. Since this bank only really needed me to stay on, John elected to offer it to Pat and me for $1.3 million. We, in turn, could sub-contract out pieces of it to whomever else we needed. Pat and I decided to bring Christy in for a more than fair percentage. Through the lawyer, Al-Hashimi, I had arranged a meeting with the head of the first private oil drilling company allowed by Saddam in Iraq. The boss was an old, former Ministry of Oil buddy of Saddam's, so no doubt, Saddam was in for a cut of the profits. Farqad, Pat, and I sold him a strategic planning exercise of sorts to organize his business for a few hundred thousand dollars. It was predicted that as a result of this process, the state-owned oil industry would become jealous and commission us to form their plans, more than likely not to lose face. These jobs, plus work I was doing for Al-Hashimi's Babalyon Commercial Bank, and couple of smaller ventures Farqad and Pat arranged with Pepsi-Cola for an organization study, amounted to around $17 million! We were elated for we had hit the big time and we knew it. Best of all, it was perfectly legal, not like the previously mentioned oil deal where we got out for fear of our lives. With all the foreign and US firms flocking to Baghdad and the amount of business going on, the Iraqis traveling abroad again, oil gushing forth from the ground, it seemed like Saddam Hussein was finally poised on history's doorstep, ready to achieve the greatness and recognition he so greedily sought from the West, or at least remake the money he blew in the war with Iran by some estimates a trillion dollars.

And then, as swiftly as it all began, it all ended. I awoke at my usual 7:00 a.m. and headed toward my room door to pick up the morning copy of my hand-delivered Baghdad Observer. In the margin was also the daily handwritten greeting from the bellboy, Mohammed, reading, "Have a nice day?" At 4:30 that morning, Iraq's army had invaded Kuwait in what the paper was calling a "police action." Saddam was claiming what he rightfully believed was the nineteenth governorate of Iraq and removing a corrupt regime, and liberating the "native Iraqi" population there. This police action was to have lasted only until that mission was accomplished and then the majority of troops would return to Iraq. Later that day, it was rumored that the process of withdrawal had begun, but no one could substantiate it. I showered and dressed hurriedly and ran down to meet my colleagues who at the time consisted of Pat, Dana (doing a pinch-hit job for the usual Citicorp manager), and Lee, my assistant. We tried to convince each other there was no need to panic and it would probably all be over within a few hours. We ate and went to the bank. The Iraqis there seemed more concerned for our fate than their own. I suggested that we forget everything we owned and head for the airport and get on any plane going any direction, for fortunately and quite coincidentally, all of us had exit visas stamped in our passports. Pat reminded us all we were still being paid and had an obligation to our respective firms to perform in a professional manner. I went ape shit! I started screaming at him, cursing loudly about priorities, the first of which was to get the fuck out of harm's way. I ordered Dana to get on the phone and get any reservation he could for himself and Lee, for Pat and I were already ticketed for Zürich. Poor Dana! He had only come over to do three weeks and look at the mess he'd gotten himself involved in! Dana could not get a line to any airline. While Pat and I were standing there arguing, an Iraqi came in and told us he had heard soldiers just grabbed seven foreigners out of their seats on the Gulf Air 8:30 a.m. flight to Bahrain and were holding them. Well, so much for that idea. I thought to myself, "fate is fate"; at least Pat and I have tickets and could hopefully fly tonight. Wrong! At 10:30 a.m., the bank informed us the airport had been closed. The events were now happening so quickly that planning, even temporarily, was useless. People were running around the hallways of the bank, scared, and crying. We started to shred documents furiously. I found it hard to concentrate on any one particular thing. When you are in the position of being dealt cards, particularly by a madman, you can only play the cards you get one card at a time.

Hussein Al-Kazaz, the bank's computer manager, requested to see me. He came into my office, very somber and in an apologetic mood. His face was a study in dejection. He and I had many battles throughout the project, but we had grown to respect each other's position, became friends and actually developed a kind of affection for each other. For certain, they not us, were the prisoners and Hussein, being in the military reserve, knew this better than most. He sat ramrod in the chair in front of my desk and rambled on, almost babbling at times, about what a tragic event this was to occur at this point in time and chalked it up to Allah. Then, he looked up and stared me straight in the eyes.

"I suppose when this is all over and you are safely home in America, that you will be a hero," he stated.

"It's possible," I said. "That is, if we get out of here alive!"

A lone tear rolled down the cheek of his handsome dark face.

"Tell them we aren't all such a bad people," he said.

I was speechless, as if this was a prophecy and I believed him. We embraced; he kissed me on both cheeks of my face and disappeared into the bowels of the bank.

At 1:30 p.m., the bank informed us they must evacuate the building as quickly as possible for it was rumored a US rocket attack on Baghdad was imminent. Now, this could really fuck up your lunch hour! We clamored around grabbing files and diskettes and I was informed that Abdullah Wahab, the bank's project director, wished to speak with me. My fights with Abdullah made my arguments with Hussein look trite by comparison. Since Abdullah controlled the purse strings, he had genuinely made my life miserable. He stood to greet me and held my hand. He was more visibly shaken than Hussein and openly crying, for he was sick, older and truly had no future. It was only years after the war I had learned Abdullah had been suffering with cancer the whole project and said nothing to anyone!

He began chokingly, "I want to tell you how deeply sorry I am for what has happened here today and for all the disagreements we had. I want you to know that I was only doing my job, and I always knew and believed in my heart that you are the very best there is at what you do in this business."

You talk about the Book of Revelation? At the eleventh hour, I get a bedside confession from Abdullah! I thought to myself, *After all this time, now he tells me this. Just as we're all about to be blasted into the afterlife!*

I hugged him and told him to take care of himself and suggested we'd better get on our way as the bank was directly across the street from an annex of the Ministry of Defense on Haifa Street and within minutes could become ground zero!

The team and I beat a quick retreat to the Sheraton, whose lobby looked like Yankee Stadium about ten minutes before a ball game. No one was missing; US and foreign businessmen, Iraqi military and government officials, embassy types, hotel bosses, you name it they were there. So far, nobody was checking hall passes.

I was told I was required to attend a briefing by a US embassy official in a meeting room in the basement of the hotel. Assembled there were the local heads of US corporations currently engaged in projects in Iraq. I later learned the speaker was Dr. Russell Smith's temporary replacement. He began, rather solemnly to read a telegram of whose content, edited by me, went something like this:

"I, George Herbert Walker Bush, President of the United States of America, do hereby order all US corporations to cease all projects undertaken in Iraq immediately. Failure to comply will result in a one million dollar fine and ten years imprisonment for every employee in violation."

I looked at Pat and said, "It's over, goodbye, seventeen million dollars!"

Well, I didn't want to be rich anyway. The dream of a lifetime had just flown out the window. The attaché informed us it would be in our best interest to remain in or near the hotel, to bide our time as best as possible and that the US embassy would do its utmost to keep us appraised of the situation as it unfolded. It was suggested that a daily briefing be given at the embassy every day at 4:30 p.m. regardless of whether or not there was anything new to report, that is if the Iraqi government approved.

The next few days were among the worst kind of hell I have ever endured. Everybody being held, at least initially, with the exception of Pat who behaved like an asshole throughout the whole ordeal, tried to remain calm and positive. We began to clash the very next morning when Pat and Dana decided there was nothing better to do than to go into work; that maybe they could organize some classes for whatever bank personnel were there on the Apple systems that we used. I wasn't by any means a flaming patriot, but this was in direct violation of an order from the President.

"And how's he going to find out?" Pat said. "Besides, it's for free!"

The meeting at the US embassy had been approved and that night the Marines and some embassy personnel came to collect us in trucks. Even at this point, not much was known. We were explained some ground rules for captivity like don't disappear without letting someone know of your whereabouts, and were read a few State Department cables about what was happening on the diplomatic front. Actually, not much as it turned out. Hedging, or posturing, is what it could be best described as.

The million-dollar question appeared to be were the borders still open and if so, which ones? It was evident that nobody from the US embassy had driven to any land border to find out and information from the British and German embassies was sketchy.

Pat and Dana went to the bank on the second and part of the third day. Bank staff had little enthusiasm for doing anything, so they gave up. I was relieved, for I was growing tired of having to cover up for their absences.

The telephones worked on a sporadic basis. You never knew during the day or night when a line would be available and if you were lucky to get through, how long the line would remain up. I managed to get through to my father and inform him of what had transpired. I said it would be better in the future if we spoke in some kind of code, for I expected the Iraqis' to soon bug the phone lines if they hadn't already! Dad was steady as always, focused on the facts and not his emotions. Shortly after that call, outgoing phone services ceased. A friend of mine, Gerry Bennett, who worked for Kindle, managed to get through from Dublin. I asked him to phone my family in the States and inform them I expected the situation to turn grave soon. My dearest friend from the States phoned. He tried to be as optimistic as possible for we had been through many trials together. My cousin Donna called to tell me she wanted me to know how much she loved me before I died! That call did not really brighten my mood.

I tried to get into some kind of pattern of living to get me through each day. The task at hand essentially was gathering news of any kind and trying to determine its accuracy and its use, or was it purely bullshit? I tried to stay away from my colleagues as much as possible for the most part, only talking to them briefly at breakfast and then reconvening to go to the daily embassy briefings. Pat was perpetually the "voice of doom and gloom," anticipating at every turn F-15s and 16s dropping out of the sky in Mach 2 dives and incinerating us or else being shot due to my relationship with Russell Smith. Lee was drunk and on medication most of the time. It was the only way he could cope. I don't think Dana fully realized what the fuck was going on. He had no global experience, let alone ever having been out of Rhode Island much. I remained in my room, trying to stay positive, trying to think of a way out of this place. I read as long as I could concentrate. I was thoroughly enjoying the Axmann Agenda, a pulp fiction about the Nazi Lebensborn program, which was set in of all places the New Jersey coast. I spent a lot of time there in my teens and had fond memories of my folks, being a hippie and early sexual experiences under the Boardwalk. It made me feel secure and grateful. At night most of the "guests" convened in the Sheraton bar to swap information, cry to each other, and get drunk, very drunk. It was my belief that this was the last option any-one needed to exercise, for if you got drunk, you got too emotional and exaggerated information as well as cloud your thinking. I started to hang out with Floyd Masoner, a US oilman who lived in Dubai. Floyd was real levelheaded and had a great sense of humor. His oil buddies were huge, macho John Wayne types who for the most part believed the Bechtel corporate jet was going to fly into Baghdad and whisk them to safety. They were all family men and when they'd get drunk would turn into blubbering fools. I loved ridiculing them, calling them fairies and pantywaists much to Floyd's ever increasing delight! They would all roar with laughter and spit beer at each other. Any one of them could have used me for a toilet brush!

As day three turned into day four, the embassy briefings were becoming more heated as well as futile. Frank Jerrel of Bechtel and Bob Bennett of Johnson Controls became our unelected spokesmen. Frank was stern and diplomatic. Bob was spontaneous and aggressive. The embassy staff had been reduced to reading all assembled State Department cables, news items, sports scores, the weather back home, etc. Bob went ballistic when informed by acting Charge d'Affairs, Joseph Smith III that our status was not that of hostage, but of "detained against our will." It was said that if exiting Iraq was possible, those holding Iraqi residence permits must remain in the country, unless they had a pre-approved exit visa. I was the only member of our team with a residence permit, even though I had an exit visa as I was going to Switzerland the day of the invasion. Bob could not confirm this nor get anyone to do it. He was also a resident and would be doomed to the same fate as me. Joe Smith said he was scheduled to meet with Saddam later in the day to inquire under what charge we were being held and why he would not reopen the airport after promising to do so for the past few days. Smith said the results of the meeting might be broadcast on the ten minutes of nightly English language news if they were still broadcasting. I left this session really scared for the first time since the ordeal began. The mood was beginning to get ugly.

Floyd suggested I join him and some British friends across the street at the Palestine Meridian to eat "Arab" pizza and drink beer. We were permitted out that far. He thought it might cheer me up after learning about the residency situation. What was formerly a beautiful Le Meridian hotel had been reduced to a cockroach infested garbage heap under Iraqi ownership and management. Nonetheless, I had a lot of laughs. We sat at a long banquet table, entertained by a very large and jovial British couple that had dedicated the remainder of their natural lives to the unrestricted consumption of food. They owned a word processing outfit and had been due to finish up a multi-year contract in a few days. Pity, now they were stuck here. Between them, they had about eight kids and were very worried about their well-being. It was clear that they were very much in love. I will never forget them. During the period that Saddam moved the remaining hostages in early December, I saw them walking hand-in-hand in the British compound on a CNN broadcast.

"I know them!" I shouted to my father.

"How?" Dad asked. "All you can see is their backs."

"Because no one in Baghdad had an ass as big as theirs, except Farqad!"

"We've got to make a plan," Pat said at breakfast the next morning. "If we are going to try to get out of Baghdad, it has to be coordinated with the precision of a military exercise."

"And how many days do you think that will take?" I asked. The dialogue between us had grown increasingly bitter.

"Oh, maybe about three or four days," he said.

"You don't say?" I said and got up to leave. By now I was having difficulty even looking at him.

We needed a plan all right and I had not only one but three. The obvious direction was by car across the desert to Jordan. King Hussein had made the wrong career move and was backing Saddam against his Arab brothers. It was to cost his people and more, the Palestinians, in ways the King could never have dreamed of at the time. He should have stuck to pussy; he had a better track record at that! Still, I considered the odds better than heading east toward Iran, particularly being an American. At least in Jordan, we might have a chance. If that attempt failed and we lived to try it again, my next plan was to go overland, north to Turkey. This was more difficult and dangerous. I had no information about what to expect at that frontier. The terrain was difficult to negotiate; the mountains, bandits and Kurdish rebels. If that failed, same conditions, I would then be out of US dollars. That left me to fend for myself. Hikmut and I had long discussions about just such a series of events occurring as did. We had developed a pre-arranged plan. If Hikmut left Baghdad it meant he was going on "vacation" to what he called "his city," the Kurdish capital of Erbil, in the mountains to the north. He would really have gone to organize his people to begin preparations to defend the city against Saddam's forces. I was to make my way by any means possible to Erbil and call a telephone number he had already provided me with, presumably some sort of safe house. Hikmut would then have collected me and stashed me in a cave in the mountains where he had hid his brothers from the draft during the war with Iran. When he could arrange it, he would bring a truck, remove the inner springs from inside the front seat, stuff me in it and then sew the bottom back in with some additional foam rubber so the driver wouldn't crush me. The driver would then head north toward Turkey. When he had gotten me within a reasonable proximity of the border, perhaps about twenty miles or so, he would let me go into the thick forest with a gun, water, a compass and some money. From that point on, it was up to me to get into Turkey. I always preferred the ocean to the mountains! Hikmut was a Kurdish extremist educated in Wales and living in Baghdad. The secret police were constantly tailing him, arresting him, and raiding his apartment, but they could never get anything on him. Why they just didn't shoot him, I'll never know as they needed no reason to do that. He was a kind, gentle man but was dedicated to the cause of the Kurdish people and avenging the atrocities against them. There was a social event held at the Mansour al-Melia Hotel in Baghdad across from the state-controlled television station. Many government officials attended the event with expensive foreign cars parked along the driveway of the hotel. Saddam and his son Uday attended it. Upon conclusion, they piled out and got in the cars, but Saddam and Uday did not travel together. The car Uday entered suddenly blew to pieces. He was not killed but paralyzed from the waist down for life. It was retribution for a psychopathic pedophile. Mrs. Saddam, traumatized by what happened to her son told Saddam, "You know that bomb was meant for you!"

I am surprised he let her live. I said to Hikmut, "Why can't you get this guy?"

All he replied was "We're trying. We're trying!"

At least now I did not have to spend any more time with Uday as when we were at the Rasheed Hotel, he was always ensconced with thugs there. If he knew I was there, he would send for me. If he saw me walked by, he would send someone after me and make me sit down with him for hours. He was a pervert, trying to impress me with tales of his exploits with underage girls who he had his people grab off the street on their way home from school, take them away in a car to his palace, and rape them. A more befitting end I couldn't think of!

Farqad finally managed to get into the hotel to see me. I had not wanted him to come, it was too dangerous, but he insisted. It was difficult to speak. He said when this was all over we would resume where we left off for the country and the people had survived an eight-year war and they were still here. I doubted seriously whether he believed his own words.

Another rumor began circulating. The hotel staff began informing its "guests" that they should begin organizing their affairs and belongings as the Iraqi authorities would be coming to remove us to other undisclosed locations.

"Shit," I thought. "Time is running out!" The window was indeed beginning to close. For those still interested, there was to be an emergency briefing at the embassy and there were cars and jeeps available to take us now. Once inside, the Marines began selling T-shirts for ten dollars a piece with "Fuq Iraq" on one side and a US Marine bulldog fucking a camel wearing Arab headgear in the ass on the other side. They recommended you not wear it if you were trying to escape! I bought a blue, sport shirt of sorts with the Marine logo and "US Embassy, Baghdad, Iraq" written on the front for twenty bucks. Semper Fidelus my behind!

Joe Smith informed us his latest diplomatic effort with Saddam had failed. Everyone there became very somber. A few women began to cry. Bob Bennett tore into a fury. He wanted to know if any embassy staff had at least driven out to the Jordanian border to see if it was still open anywhere along the frontier. No one had; they had all been too preoccupied with "matters of State." It was suggested someone go to the Jordanian embassy to find out. Someone had; it was closed. Bennett said he had checked the State Department "rule book" and any US embassy worldwide in the event of conflict was required to provide any US citizen requesting it with transportation, a member of the US embassy staff to accompany them and money to escape with. Smith said they didn't have enough vehicles, did not have any money and did not recommend any embassy support as this may "jeopardize" any opportunity to escape.

"Well, then what the fuck are you prepared to do?" somebody shouted out, the crowd now borderline lynch mob.

"I recommend you try to get out of Iraq by any means available at your disposal, at the earliest possible convenience!" Smith said.

There you have it, the official State Department policy. Your government in action, your tax dollars hard at work! I had often wondered over the years if all the stories I heard about the incompetence in our Federal bureaucracy were true or if it was just people pissing and moaning, because they weren't getting their "fair share." After this unbelievable display of a total misapplication of logic, there no longer remained any doubt in my mind. What were we supposed to do, rob a bank and thumb a lift out? The moment you have all waited for was finally here. Yes, in the eyes of your government, the same pocket protector guys who process your IRS returns, you are expendable! One hysterical woman asked if we could take shelter inside the embassy compound. She must have had hallucinations of the fall of Saigon in her head where huge choppers from some carrier would land on the roof and lift the women and children to safety. Sure, we were welcome to take refuge in the embassy, but nobody was certain for how long for they had just received orders to evacuate non-essential staff and hoped to close the compound within seventy-two hours. It was definitively the conclusion of the diplomatic process. On the way out of the building, Joe Smith asked if I'd seen the television broadcast of him and Saddam. I indeed had caught the brief snippet they showed.

"Did I look Kissingeresque?" he wanted to know.

"To me, you looked scared out of your fucking wits!" I said.

It was the last time I would visit the US Embassy. We were now left to our own devices. The old sacrificial lamb story.

Back at the hotel, I was going nowhere fast trying to convince my team we needed to look at doing something to save ourselves, whatever it was to be, a whole lot faster than we thought. Pat was still fighting me all the way, insisting we had to plan this carefully. I had lost all patience with him and "officially" informed him if the chance arose to get out; I was going to take it, with or without any of them. Lee kept tugging at me, saying he needed to talk to me privately. He was drunk and most annoying. The sun had begun its slow summer descent; a big, beautiful orange clock. I heard Frank Jerrell and some of the Bechtel guys were going to try a run for Jordan in the middle of the night. I found him in the chaos of the bar and asked if he had any room for one more. He said he doubted it, but would phone me later if a space became available. He never did. Lee kept pressing his demand to talk to me. I brushed him away and went to seek out Ramadan, our daily taxi driver, in front of the hotel. Ramadan's son, a pleasant but fiery ex-soldier, told us his father was home drunk, as he usually was at this time of the day. As a matter of record, Ramadan was drunk everyday almost all day, primarily for the same reason as Johnson David!

"Look," I began. "I have a proposition for you."

"Yes, Mr. John, for you, anything at all," he said.

"For more money than its worth, will Pop drive us to the border with Jordan?" I asked.

He grew animated. He must have smelled the money in my pocket. He knew we paid his father well for when his father was busy the son would drive us daily to the bank. The money was all the same for they all lived together as one, large family.

"I'm sure he would," he replied. "He's already been approached by others. When were you thinking of going?"

"I'm not sure," I said. "Maybe in two or three days. I'll tell you for certain tomorrow morning so don't book anyone else until I tell you when."

"As you like, Mr. John, and if my father does not take you, I will be happy to take you," he smiled.

"Do you know anything about the Turkish border?" I asked him.

"Oh, Mr. John, very dangerous. Too many bridges with check-points. Is much better to go to Jordan," he concluded. Well, that iced it. Whenever it was, Jordan was where!

Lee was now becoming more than a minor irritation. He insisted on talking to me to the point of being belligerent. By now the day was ending. I was running out of time and still had more people to see. I agreed to speak to him if not for anything but to get rid of him. Lee and I walked over to the country club which was directly next door to the hotel where I had so many delightful lunches with Hashimi and Farqad. Al-Hashimi, who was on the Board of Directors of the club had arranged for me to use the facility anytime I wanted. The gardens were magnificent and it was a safe haven to talk.

We grabbed a small table away from anyone else and ordered a round of drinks, not that Lee needed another one. He had drunk consistently throughout the project, not that I could entirely blame him for the boredom at times was maddening. But he had increased his consumption rate steadily, particularly over the past two months to the point where I would call it heavy. Lee had also been on multiple medications as well, the most serious of these drugs being Prozac. He was a veritable medicine chest of tranquilizers, anti-depressants, barbiturates, and more. He was certainly beyond dopey. He ignored my many warnings.

"Okay," I said. "What's the trauma that can't wait?" I asked him hurriedly.

He sat there with that smug, preppy look I detested, an extra-length cigarette between two fingers, jingling his ice cubes.

He said to me, almost comically, "I don't really know where to begin or quite how to tell you."

"Lee," I said, trying to remain controlled. "If we are going to get out of here, I need all the time I can get and I know something more serious may happen to us in the next twenty-four hours so."

"That's just it," Lee said. "We may not be going anywhere."

"Do you know something I don't know, or are we just pretending you're a diplomat?" I asked him.

Then he dropped it. "I've been gathering intelligence for the Defense Intelligence Agency (the intel unit of the US military) since January," he said.

I really hoped he was just loaded and exaggerating something very remotely attached to what he just told me. Exploding right now would do me little good for I needed to determine quickly if he was lying, although I wouldn't know what motive he'd have and if he wasn't, how big of a problem I really had to deal with.

"Go ahead, Lee, explain it to me as accurately as you can," I asked him.

"Well over Christmas holiday, I met up with an old buddy from Georgetown University at a party, a guy who I had not seen in a long time," he began. "It turns out after grad school he went to work for the DIA. I told him what we were doing here and we made a date to get together. It was then that he asked me to gather information about Baghdad, you know, for the good of the country, my patriotic duty, fly the flag and all that bullshit!" By now, he was becoming galvanized on his explanation. I had long worried that Lee might be bait for the intelligence community for he fit the stereotype perfectly with all the qualifications they liked to recruit. Specifically, a snob, wealthy, gay, and thrill junkies. Lee also ran on the fringe of the Beltway circles so I knew he might be fair prey.

"What did they want to know? What did you give them?" I asked him, now more curious than angry.

"I provided them mostly with information about street layouts, landmarks, important buildings; the kind of info you could pick up simply by performing our daily routine. I'd also go walking in sections of the city on our day off," he continued.

"And what form did the information take?" I asked.

"Oh, uh, photographs, drawings, diagrams, cassettes. Basically everything but video," he answered.

"Jesus Christ, Lee, is that it, I mean did you miss anything?" I screamed.

He just sat there with his head bowed.

"When was the last point of contact?" I wanted to know.

"About two months back. I told him I didn't want to take the risk anymore," he said.

It was useless to chastise him about his selfishness in terms of the risk he put us all in. It would not have accomplished a thing right now. To borrow a line from Moe Howard of the *Three Stooges*, "Remind me to kill you later!"

I remained composed and continued what had developed into an interrogation.

"So we've got some breathing room since the last point of contact, that's good," I said.

He looked up now for the first time in a while.

"John, that isn't the worst of it," he said. I started to shake a little, for I became terrified over what he might tell me next.

"The other day, I went looking in one of my bags (he had an entire wardrobe with him) for a certain book. In the book, I kept the card of my DIA contact. It had his name, address, and phone number, everything on it. The card was gone! I've searched everywhere. It's the only thing in all my belongings that is missing, so I presume someone purposely took it."

Brilliant fucking deduction, you idiot! I thought to myself.

"Was it a Washington, DC, address?" I was afraid to ask.

"No, it was Tel Aviv," he said.

I wanted to be sick, but luckily, I hadn't eaten in hours. If we had even a chance to begin with of getting out, this certainly would have ended it, permanently.

"Listen," Lee said. "I'll just stay behind and you guys go for it. If we got stopped, they'd arrest us all." This was to be his token apology.

"Who else have you told?" I asked.

"Nobody. I was thinking maybe we should tell Sam. Possibly he could advise us?" Sam had been Dr. Tomasz's former partner who just happened to be in Baghdad when the invasion occurred. Sam, like the Doctor, was also an Iraqi-American. Sam had been trying to get a meeting with the Minister of the Interior in a last ditch attempt to gain the freedom of all those being "detained against their will." I did not want to do anything to jeopardize what little opportunity he might have. I quickly decided it was best if no one else knew at all.

"No, Lee, let's not do that. In fact, let's not tell anyone, especially Pat, he'll freak!" I ordered him. "I'm not leaving Baghdad without you. You are a bigger risk if you stay here. At least if we're moving, they will have to find us first."

"And if they do, they will kill us," he implored.

"If they don't, I'm going to kill you myself!" I said.

We walked back to the hotel. I hung out in the bar for as long as I could stand the commotion. There wasn't any more substantial news to evaluate, just more rumors. I decided to retire for the night. It was best to try to get as much sleep as possible, to stay rested, and conserve energy. As I lay there on my bed, I resigned myself to the fact that I was going to die. I tried to focus on what that meant. I was never going to get married, never have any children, not get to see my nephews grow into men, never see my dad again. No, I wasn't going to be around for any of those things. I couldn't believe my luck had finally run out. I wanted to live more now than at any time in my past and I didn't even have a say in it. I wondered where the soul really went. When I was a kid, St. Joseph's church in Oradell, New Jersey, where I grew up, had a huge marble wall behind the altar. When you died, I thought you just went behind that wall. That was where heaven was, where my beloved grandfather went after being so mercilessly ravaged from cancer. But now, there was a pall within my soul, like it was raining inside me for my entire belief system, my faith in God, had been shattered. I wondered what my family was going through; how torturous this must be for them. At least I knew where I was, they didn't. The reality that angered me most was not Saddam, nor Bush, not even what Lee had just told me. It was that I was going to die for the glory of corporate America, for the glory of the firm. A company so cruel and greedy, so full of pretentious assholes that shortly after my death they'd be figuring a way out of not paying the insurance benefits. No one in the Washington office or the headquarters in New York had even bothered to try to contact us when numerous other firms had at least managed one phone call in to their employees. I could see them all in DC, talking to New York, determining which of them should dazzle the morons in the State Department with their own "armchair general's" view on the situation in the Gulf. It would be a fight to determine who had the biggest ego to satiate. What a waste, they won't even remember my name two weeks from now. Most likely they will be figuring out how to bill the Rasheed Bank for my time right up to the exact minute of my death!

I was beginning to seethe and grow nervous which is not conducive to sleeping. This had gone far enough, time to turn it off. I felt like I was looking over the edge into insanity and one more step, one more thought, would push me over the brink. I managed to fall into a sleep, more from mental exhaustion that anything else.

Sometime in the night I awoke suddenly to the deafening roar of cannon fire. I bolted upright in the bed.

"This is it," I thought. "It's showtime!"

Another salvo erupted. I jumped out of the bed in the dark, looking for my pants. Jesus, I didn't want to be this high up in the building. I kept the lights off, found a shirt, and my sneakers and pulled them on. Another blast; I hit the floor. I crawled on my belly to the window, pulled the drapes slightly apart and peered out into the Baghdad night. Again, the cannon fired and the glass shook. But I could not see anything. No illumination in the sky, no fire. The city looked at peace. The rumble ceased. I waited for some time and exhausted, went back to bed. You kind of reach that "fuck them; let them kill me" frame of mind. Only later the next day, was I to find out the cannon was to commemorate the precise moment the Iraq-Iran cease-fire was declared the previous year! Just like the Arabs to do something like that in the dead of the night. I felt like a jerk.

CHAPTER 8

Midnight at the Oasis

The telephone rang at 6:00 a.m. It was Frank Jerrell from Bechtel on the other end. I was surprised to hear his voice. I didn't even think he knew my name. He was calling to tell me he was leaving Baghdad and that I needed to get out of Iraq as soon as possible. Gee, thanks Frank, tell me something I didn't know! The phone rang again. It was the US Embassy. They were calling to inform me the situation was indeed grave and they had information which led them to believe the "detainees" were going to be herded up and moved into a single compound with specific people moved out to strategic Iraqi military installations as "human shields." I had always wanted to go on a turkey shoot! They advised me to get out of Iraq immediately through any means available and if I managed to solve that puzzle, could I please let them know I was going so they could keep score. Well, this was going to be a great day and it was only 7:00 a.m.! I'd had two warnings and I was wide awake. I wondered what was next. The telephone rang again. Unbelievably, it was my father. He'd been up all night trying to get a line and finally found some operator who was sympathetic enough to connect him. God works in strange and mysterious ways! Dad told me that later in the day President Bush was giving a major policy speech about the invasion of Kuwait and what immediate and future action was going to be taken by the United States and the United Nations toward Iraq. It would also more than likely contain a scathing credibility attack against Saddam, which was likely to piss him off big time! That address, if it weren't decided already, would certainly seal the fate of all those foreigners that remained. If there was a chance any borders were still open, this condemnation would certainly close them. I told Dad in the event I could get a line still open, I would call him and tell him I was going on vacation to a specific spot as yet undecided and I would send him a postcard when I got settled. This way he would know I was going to make a run for it and where I was trying to get to. I also added that in the event he did not hear from me for a couple of days that he should not worry for it did not necessarily mean the worse. I told him I loved him and hung up. It was time to go!

I showered and put on the most comfortable and durable clothes I had for I feared I would be in them for a very long time. I went down to the restaurant to get some breakfast. It was now about 8:30. As I walked in I saw Pat, Dana, and Lee already there, talking to a huge oil guy, appropriately named Tex and a Brit and his girlfriend, oddly enough named Dick and Jane! I got some food and listened while they went through a litany of various plans; tactics and schemes, what was involved and how long they would take to develop. When I'd had my fill of them and breakfast, I informed them of Bush's impending speech and what impact it may present. Remarkably, they listened. I said I did not care what any of them were going to do but as soon as I could organize it that I was leaving, and if any of them wanted to go they were welcome to join me. Everyone, with no hesitation, wanted to go. I sent Lee and Dana to go buy water with what few dinars they had between them. Bottled water and any canned soft drinks they could find. I told the waiter, another Palestinian I had nurtured, to go find me as many hard-boiled eggs as he could. Pat asked me what I was planning to do with them. I said I didn't know when or if we were going to eat again and these would have to tide me over. He laughed at me. Tex had a pickup truck and someone to drive it so we could dump our belongings in it. I didn't care about luggage. I just wanted out.

"Tex," I said. "What's your real name?"

He poked the brim of his cowboy hat back, peered down at me like a mighty oak about to fall and replied, "Clarence Abernathy II!"

It was hard to picture someone this grizzly being named "Clarence." I liked him a lot. He was calm and rational. He also spoke fluent Arabic, specifically a dialect from the west of Iraq, straight where we were heading.

I went outside to find Ramadan. He was nowhere in sight. Neither was his son. Another driver, a young man whose English was excellent, told me that Ramadan had taken two men to the border early this morning.

"Jerrell," I thought. "He nicked my driver. Now I'm fucked!"

"Can I be of some assistance?" the man inquired.

I looked him up and down. I didn't have many alternatives.

"Come across the street with me," I asked him. Iraqi soldiers and government types were beginning to mill around the front of the Sheraton and I did not want the risk of being overheard.

"Will you drive me to the Jordanian frontier?" I asked him.

"Yes, yes I will," he replied. "Just you?"

"No," I said. "There are seven."

"We'll need two cars, plus one additional for back-up," he continued.

"Three?" I shouted. "Where will we get two more?"

"It's all right," he said. "I have two brothers and they each have cars. It's perfect."

And now, the $64,000 question. "How much," I asked him, hoping for mercy.

"Three hundred US dollars a car," he stated very firmly.

At the black market price of three to one, each car had the buying power of $1,000 dollars. That's $3,000 for a taxi ride, literally the ride of a lifetime, or the end of it! In some places, the exchange went as high as five to one. I couldn't blame him. They were risking their lives for money. If we made it, they still had to live there. They would be hanged for an offense such as this and more than likely, the remainder of their family would be threatened or killed. This is Saddam's way. Charming man, isn't he?

"Deal," I said. "You get your brothers together, fill the tanks with gas, check the oil, water, tires, and Freon for the air conditioner."

We would melt to death in the desert without A/C. I told him to be ready to go by 11:00 and went back to the hotel. The Sheraton manager, a former boxer from the University of Oklahoma who had been a good friend to us, grabbed a hold of me and told me that government officials would likely begin relocating the "guests" in the afternoon and I should get my people organized to go. I wanted him to tell me this was certain, but all he replied was "en es Allah." Right, "in your ear" was more likely!

Pat and I argued whether to pay our hotel bill. I wanted to leave them open for if we did not get out and lived, we'd have a place to return to even for just one night. This was particularly relevant to me since I was the only one with a residence permit and might not be allowed out regardless. Pat, being the loyal bureaucrat he is, insisted we complete our corporate responsibility in good faith and pay the bill. I was in no mood to fight him any further. If I came back, I would probably go to prison and what the fuck did I care; we all had corporate American Express cards anyway so the firm owned the liability regardless. I even paid Dana's bill for he had no plastic at all. Where we found these rubes from I'll never know. How did they think the world worked anyway? Pat said he was going to try to reach John P. in New York, that maybe through Citibank he could arrange some kind of support from their operation in Amman if we made it that far. It was the first useful suggestion he had in the whole process. For some unexplained reason, telephone service overseas had become readily available. We went our separate ways to pack. I went to my room and placed a call with the hotel operator to my father in North Carolina. Then I began the process of purging any non-essential items. Out went the computer diskettes, plans, reports, diagrams, books, and pictures, anything that might call attention to me at the border. The less assuming you are the better. I parted company with a "Fuq Iraq" T-shirt that had been given to me and was praying the rest of them had the good sense to do so as well. I managed to condense everything I had into two duffle bags. Hurriedly, I wrote a letter to Mayada. I wanted to tell her I loved her. She had a right to know and deserved to know this. Then I took my empty Samsonite suitcase and taped the letter to the inside and locked it.

Move faster, I thought.

The next thing was to call Farqad and of all the inopportune times not to be home, he wasn't. At least I got his son Akmed on the phone who spoke English and not Bessrad, who didn't. Akmed was the Arab version of Pugsly Addams, the kind of fat kid who had ice cream stains all over his shirt like Pugsly used to. Akmed started crying that I was leaving. He probably was thinking, *Gee, there goes my candy connection!*

"Akmed, tell your father I am leaving a gray Samsonite suitcase with his name on the outside for him to pick up at the Sheraton," I explained.

"The combination to the lock is 192." That was the first three digits of the year my father was born, 1927, which was also the only way I could remember his birthday.

"Tell Farqad to deliver the letter inside to Mayada Khadim at the Rasheed Bank."

I had previously introduced the two of them just in the event anything like what had just occurred did and told Mayada whatever it was she needed that Farqad would take care of her per my instructions to him.

"Okay, Akmed? You got that?" I asked him.

"Okay, Uncle John, I tell him right away. Goodbye and I love you," Akmed choked out.

Jesus, I felt bad, as if they were going to lead me down the hall and strap me in the electric chair. Mayada phoned just as Pat walked in my room, making circular hand gestures to get going; that we were running behind. I didn't have much of a timetable to speak of, but I did not want to hit the border after Bush gave his speech for fear of what may break out as a result, nor did I want to arrive in the dark. I hated the dark. Ever since I was a little kid I hated the dark.

What I had long waited to tell Mayada I couldn't, not with Pat standing around. She assumed we were going to take a chance at leaving, and wanted to say goodbye. All I could tell her was about the letter and to be expecting it. Opening a medicine bottle, I took a handful of Lomotil.

Pat said, "What are you taking so many for, are you sick?"

"No," I said. "If they shoot me I don't want to shit in my pants!"

"Hey, what else you got?" Pat said, poking his nose around the bathroom.

"Xanax," I replied. "Need some?"

Pat gulped down a few. I didn't, as I had not taken any in Iraq. I just had them more as a precautionary measure. I was bound and determined to do this au naturel. Besides, fear was enough of a high as it was!

The operator rang with my father on the line.

"Dad," I said. "We've decided to leave for vacation a little earlier than planned. As a matter of fact, we're going in an hour or so." My father knew, as we had previously arranged, exactly what to say.

"And where are you going?" he asked.

"We've decided to go to Jordan for a few days. I'll send you a postcard when I get there," I told him.

"Well, have a safe trip and good luck, son," Dad replied and that was all as the line was cut.

It was one of the most eerie feelings I've ever had. I could just picture my mother and father sitting and waiting for a call to say I made it or I'm dead!

We arrived back at the front desk, ready to assemble, and depart. The clerk handed me the telephone. It was a young lady from the US Embassy wanting to know our status and if any Iraqi had approached me about leaving the hotel.

"No," I said. "As a matter of fact, we are about to go on vacation to Jordan. Would you like me to send you a postcard from there?" I asked.

"If it's possible, that would be great," she said.

The pickup was loaded with all the bags and tied down by Tex and the driver. Tex was financing that part of the expedition. The Brits had no money. Typical, they must have been Scots. I asked my guys for their money. I knew they didn't have any either.

I looked at Pat and said, "Well, I guess you're staying."

"Hey, wait a minute John." He grew upset as I hoped he would.

I had my fill of his shit, not just recently, but from the beginning of the project. If not for his interference and insistence, I could have been managing an oil project off the coast of Venezuela. I tore him a new asshole, screaming at his state of unpreparedness. How could he or the others think they were ever going to get out with no money? It was cruel of me to do, but at least I had part of it out of my system. My nerves had begun to get the best of me. I still had Lee and his intelligence activities to contend with. Fortunately, I had been hoarding my money to buy a Rolex on the black market for far cheaper than their normal retail price. And my boss back in Washington wanted to know why I wanted a bag with ten grand in it? I figured I was becoming a decent geopolitical analyst. A lot of good it was going to do me now. To be right and dead was not my objective.

The drivers wanted me to meet their father. He was the building engineer at the Palestine Meridian Hotel across the street. He told me his sons were good boys and they would look out for us. I told him if anything went wrong as a result of their deliberate actions and I lived to tell about it, that I would come back and kill him. I had never uttered these words before to any human being in my life. I felt totally calm, like I had said them one hundred times before. Maybe I had gone over the edge and didn't know it.

The man just stared at me and gulped. Nobody said a word.

"Let's go," I commanded and our desert caravan loaded up and limped out onto the street. As we headed toward the city center, a strange thought occurred to me. I wondered to myself where in this vast wasteland I was going to sleep tonight? It was the first time in my life that I truly didn't know the answer. The brothers had not had the time to gas their cars as I requested so we pulled into a large service station that was teeming with Iraqi military. I was furious.

"What a great fucking start!" I said to Lee, for I had put him in the same car with me for safekeeping.

"Why don't we just go up to the soldiers and give ourselves up?" I said.

On top of it, there was a long queue for gas. There was no choice in the matter. It had to be done. We stayed down low in the car while the brothers went about their business.

After what seemed like an eternity, we were on our way again. The procession didn't get very far. Shortly after pulling out on the highway, one of the cars got a flat tire. We pulled underneath an over-pass where it would be cooler and darker. We had to unload all the contents in the trunk to discover none of the spare tires in any car fit the wheel the flat was on. I didn't for a second ever know why it ever occurred to me that any of them would! One car lost, no refund. We lost some precious time dicking around with this problem. Again, the caravan commenced. The highway was a good road. There was significant troop movement in the outskirts of the city, but nothing I considered alarming. As we left the city limits, we made a series of turns as the highway, what there was of it, abruptly ended and that we needed to get on the road that would take us straight across the desert to the border. At this perimeter, there was a lot of anti-aircraft artillery pointed skyward, larger than the popguns on the banks of the Tigris River. Another "Kodak moment" shot to hell I thought. I craned my head around to see how the rest of my crew was getting on and noticed somehow the truck with Dick and Jane was no longer trailing. Our driver suggested they possibly took an alternative road for there was one that ran to the same destination we were going that was parallel to the road we were on about five kilometers away. It sounded reasonable, but I really didn't care whether they or our luggage showed up. Once we had clearance to cross, Iraq was history, at least for this lifetime. The road to Al-Rouashid was a two-lane blacktop running west across the desert as far as the eye could see. Unless we were intercepted, this was as eventful as the ride was going to get. Trucks had grooved the road from their weight in the melting sun, so you put your two front tires in and "rode the rails." One only had to be careful of the high spots, as it would be easy to rip out an oil pan, transmission or rear axle.

I was hungry. I gave Lee and the driver each an egg and hoarded one for when we got closer to the border. We didn't speak very much. I didn't have much to say. I believe fear was numbing Lee and me. We chained smoked Marlboro Red 100s. I was oblivious to how strong they were since I had only smoked "lights" for years. The good news is I survived the Iraqis. The bad news is I'd die of lung cancer!

The only point of panic came when I dropped my cigarette lighter between the cracks in the rear seat cushion and could not retrieve it.

"Oh great," I said. "How are we fixed for matches?"

Lee said, "One book. One of us will have to keep a cigarette going at all times."

Of course, the cigarette lighter in the car didn't work. After a while, this posed no difficulty as Lee was smoking literally one after the other.

After a couple of hours, we reached a small village and took a brief pit stop. Again, more soldiers everywhere while we were checking the necessities. I noticed out of the corner of my eye Ramadan, our loyal driver, heading back to Baghdad in the opposite direction.

"Well," I said to no one in particular. "At least I know where he got off to." Since his taxi was empty, whomever he took either got through, was captive again or dead.

The only scenery of interest was numerous radar outposts, surrounded by twelve-foot high hurricane fences and barbed wire. I suspected these were the locations some of the "human shields" would be moved to. Out here, following the road in the middle of nowhere, they would be sitting ducks for any aircraft.

The first sign for the border appeared. "Al-Rouashid, seventy kilometers," it said. A reality check if ever there was one. We decided to pull over for a leak. Traffic was increasing in both directions, especially toward Baghdad. Convoys of big, flatbed trucks with tarps pulled down tight over penis-like cylinders. I did not need to consult my "rules of engagement" handbook to figure out what they were! The heat was staggering to the point the hot air burned your lungs. As there is a definitive lack of trees or large bushes in the desert, you just had to let it all hang out. If James Dean could take a piss in front of a thousand people while filming "Giant," then I could manage this. Ah, how do you spell r-e-l-i-e-f? Toward the conclusion of this exercise, not paying attention I pissed on my pant leg and on one sneaker. The heat was so intense that they dried almost instantly. Glad I didn't have to take a shit!

Al Rouashid, fifty kilometers. I wished that this ride would last forever, that we could just go on and on. I did not want to face what I believed was to be my destiny. Al-Rouashid, forty kilometers! I reached into my pants pocket for my pill bottle of Xanax. Should I pop a few, just to stay calm? The situation certainly was justified. No, better to be aware of my senses. Lee was foraging around in a bag and I could hear the rattle of pills.

"Just something to soothe my nerves," he said.

"Here, hold these with your shit," I asked him. It never dawned on him to inquire why.

"Sure, whatever," he said.

I figured if the Iraqis took his bag and accused him of drug trafficking, better they shoot him for the whole lot than me for one measly bottle!

Al-Rouashid, thirty kilometers! My mind was a mass of unconnected thoughts, but surprisingly clear. I recall thinking about the Jews heading toward Auschwitz, looking out the boxcar windows, going toward what was to be certain death. Going to a place where there would be no escape, only finality. I had to be hopeful. At least we had a chance.

Al-Rouashid, twenty kilometers! The mood in the car was intensely somber until I burst out laughing.

"What could you find to be so damn funny at a time like this?" Lee asked.

Not knowing whether to be sacred or not, I ceased convulsing and smiled.

"All our lives we are taught to obey laws, behave, be Christian and pray so that we can control our lives for the better so we can get to heaven," I said.

Lee was puzzled as I expected, probably thinking I slipped into the initial stage of shock or madness.

We flashed past the ten-kilometer road sign and as flat as the landscape was, we could see the building that was to hold our fate, sitting there in the stillness, like Auschwitz.

"We think we have control," I continued. "But only God will determine our fate."

"We are going into that building and either die or come out the other side free. And there is no other choice. We have no influence whatsoever. It is entirely God's will and there is not a thing we're going to do about it!"

My spirit began to sink for I realized the odds were not good.

"For any man to believe he has control of his destiny, the time in which to leave his life, is utterly ridiculous. I find it hysterical to realize all these years I could have thought any different," I said.

Maybe the moment of faith occurs only at the instant of impending death. I was at peace with myself; comfortable in knowing I did the best I could, thankful for the opportunities I had. And finally, it was time, our time. I looked at Lee, whom fright had by now consumed, and said, "Let's rock 'n' roll. And keep your mouth shut!"

As we approached the first gate, heavily armed soldiers appeared from every direction, thrusting their guns in the car window. Our driver asked for our passports and slipped them out to one guard who appeared to inspect them studiously. I noted the time, five o'clock in the evening. He nodded to the gatekeeper who lifted the crossbar and we drove through.

"Is that it? Are we clear?" I jumped with anticipation.

"No," replied the driver. "We have just entered the border compound, that's all."

I felt like a fool. There's no way it's going to be this easy. Car number two with Pat, Dana, and Tex followed us in. The scene that ensued was something from a DeMille spectacle. Camped out on the opposite side of the road that ran through the compound were thousands of people who, I was told, were waiting clearance to cross into Jordan. All of them were Arabs, Kuwaitis, Jordanians, nomads, you name it. They had constructed a makeshift town of sorts, something that resembled ages past and were prepared to hunker down for the duration. We parked the cars in a parking lot in front of a very long, two-story concrete building. This was the headquarters for customs, visas, road taxes, etc. It was obviously under control of the army, who were in turn running government clerks. After a brief stretch, I walked over to an Arab man leaning against an American station wagon. We gave each other the once over. I elected the direct approach and walked straight toward him. He grinned a toothless smile, looked around and said softly, "Lift, mister, Amman?"

"How much?" I inquired.

"How many?" he replied.

"Seven," I said. "Plus baggage."

"One hundred American dollars," he said.

"A piece?" I quickly asked.

"No, the lot of you," he said.

I told him we might be a while if at all and not to go anywhere, just to stay put. *Great*, I said to myself. *That's the other leg of the journey booked.*

There was no sign of any Citibank people. As we approached what I guessed was the main office, Saddam Hussein was in the middle of his response to George Bush's speech, which I assumed had been broadcast earlier. Saddam was in a lather, blaring at the highest decibel from every speaker in the compound. He sounded like some ominous voice of doom speaking from somewhere in the beyond. Everyone in my immediate vicinity stood motionless. I looked at Pat.

"Nothing like perfect, fucking timing," I said. If ever we could have picked a worse moment to arrive, the precise circumstances I was trying to avoid, this was it! We went inside the building and slipped our passports through a slot in the glass to an official. He gave them a cursory glance, passed them back and told us we must wait until "His Excellency" concludes his address. I pulled up a slab of concrete and slumped to the floor. The rhetoric seemed endless. I smoked. I talked to Tex. I smoked some more. Abruptly, automatic weapons fire broke out beyond the front door. It was loud and it was close. Pat looked at me and said, "Now I really wish they would quit that!" I thought the situation was beginning to affect his mind. If I sat there guessing any longer as to its origin, I might find myself the subject of it. How easily it would have been for any of them to burst in the door, train their weapons on us, and fire. And no one would have been the wiser, no explanation required. Just dispose of the bodies and report we disappeared in the desert. Our government wouldn't have given a shit, just one more report to fill out. Pat followed me out the door as curiosity got the better of me. There stood a soldier, a Major I believe, laughing loudly and firing a gun the size of a Browning automatic rifle into the air. He was aiming randomly at the crowd camped across the street. He peeked a side-glance at me, dipped his weapon and shifted his weight in my direction. My fucking asshole puckered and I gasped! He shifted again and continued firing. I didn't realize I'd gotten a bit too close, not even when the shells were plinking off my head and chest. Saddam kept screaming, "Allahu Akbar, Allahu Akbar," or "God is the greatest." As opposed to women's ululating shrill at Arab weddings, this was the military's version of cutting loose.

"Ah, they're probably blanks," Pat said.

"You think so?" I replied.

I knew he was trying to humor himself and probably me. Another officer came over and said loosely translated, "Cut that shit out!" He took the weapon and walked away. I went closer and scooped up a handful of spent shells. They were Russian. This could be a good bargaining chip if we ever got to the question of my bonus for doing this job.

Pat and I went back in to maintain our vigil. The sun was beginning to set. The pick-up with Dick and Jane arrived and they had joined Dana and Tex. On the faces of the many Arabs we waited with, hopelessness had become the order of the day.

When the visa office opened again there was a mad convergence by all in this tiny room. Arms and hands from every direction thrust passports of every color through the tiny slot in the glass partition. Tex was huge and managed to barrel his way to the front with me stuck right up his behind. We were told to sit and wait. More cigarettes; more idle chitchat. The official in charge began to call our names one by one. All of us were given permission to leave. I hurriedly leafed through my passport to read the proof myself. It was there, the exit stamp. I heard from sources that had I not previously been issued an exit/re-entry visa by the Baghdad police to go to Switzerland, I would not have been permitted to leave Iraq because of my status as a resident. You talk about coincidence! I was flush with excitement, but it was to be short lived.

"Let's get the fuck out of here!" I shouted when we were a safe distance from the crowd still converging on the office. I looked around for my man with the station wagon.

"No," Pat said. "We can't leave yet. First we have to get the bags and clear customs."

"Are you nuts?" I screamed at him. "Screw the luggage, we're free to go! I have a car all set to leave."

We walked around the back of the customs hall to wait for the pick-up to be cleared to enter the area. Our drivers from Baghdad wanted to take us to Amman, for more money of course, but the Iraqis' denied them permission to enter Jordan. They tried to bribe the official in charge but that did not work. I thanked them for their help and gave them most of the Iraqi dinar I had left as a tip, even though they ripped me off for the car with the flat tire. Besides, the currency wasn't worth the paper to wipe your ass with outside of Iraq and I couldn't find any Monopoly games in progress! They left us to return to Baghdad and we were totally on our own, just the Iraqi military and us. Cozy little group, yes?

After unloading the pickup and sending it back to Baghdad, we paraded all of our possessions into the customs hall and put them up on a counter. I held my hands together so they wouldn't see them shaking. The officials were after everything we had already disposed of, especially any photographs. After a fruitless but thorough search, they dismissed us all with the wave of a hand. I truly thought this was the last obstacle to freedom but it wasn't. By now, it was growing increasingly dark which was another fear as shit always happens in Iraq in the night. Any minute I expected the Iraqis' to inform us that Saddam had sealed all the borders shut, probably resultant of whatever American threats were made in the last few hours. It was a race against time and the unexpected. As a result of Pat's decision, we were now without a driver and forced to wait for Citibank to show up, that's if they ever got any message at all. The crowd was thinning out as dinner hour approached.

"Hey, you got any of those eggs left?" Pat asked. I could hear his stomach growl a mile away.

"Sure," I said with a smirk.

"Can I have one," he inquired.

"Fifty bucks," was my price.

"Aw, c'mon, I haven't eaten anything since breakfast," he pleaded. "You know I don't have any money."

This provided me yet another opportunity to rail into him about having to finance the escape, the customs decision and now, no ride to anywhere.

He turned away dejected for this had become pure folly for me and I was no longer amused by any of it, but I was less than amused by Pat.

I gave him the egg.

It was now time for one experience I had been dreading but could no longer put off, the bathroom. Much to my chagrin, I only had to pee. I headed for the bathroom on the other side of the hall. I approached it cautiously, as was always best to do in the Arab world. As is the custom in the Middle East, it was only a hole in the ground with a watering can next to it to pour down the crack of your ass. However, this particular hole had long overflowed and piss and shit were everywhere. Rolling up my pant legs and taking a deep gulp of air, I ventured in and relieved myself. I walked outside, swatted the last few flies that had rest on me and saw Lee approaching.

"Where's the bathroom, I gotta shit real badly!" he winced.

"Around the corner, can't miss it," I said.

"Is it passable?" he wanted to know.

"No problem," was all I said as I burst out laughing.

In the interim, the people from Citibank miraculously arrived. "Ahmed" was head of security for the Citibank Amman branch. The other man was his driver. Ahmed had gotten the call from John in New York. They could only guess at our time of arrival at the outpost. He apologized endlessly for the delay. Good, I thought, enough of this crap, let's go! Ahmed explained there was one problem; there were two more cars coming and he didn't know where he had lost them on the way out through the desert. We would have to wait for we could not fit all the people and the luggage in one car.

An official came over and asked to check our passports. We showed him and he walked away. This was not a good sign. It was now pitch dark and the guard had rotated to a new crew. There was even a greater military presence than before. The window of opportunity was slowing closing around us. We could now have been safely gone hours ago. The longer you expose yourself to a situation such as this the greater to chance of something going seriously wrong and we were already well beyond the odds. Sooner or later, someone is going to come along who knows what he is doing with the authority to do it and we're fucked!

The other Citibank cars arrived. We began to pack the trunks with all the aplomb of a family of idiots going to the beach for vacation. We created quite a ruckus, arguing with each other over what goes where and who sits where in which car. To add to this confusion, Pat picked up two more American businessmen who managed to get through and were stranded without a lift. One, Kevin from Boston, had drunk a quart of whiskey and a six-pack of beer before leaving Baghdad and was extremely drunk. Naturally, he was Irish. Surely as I expected, the curtain was about to drop on our little charade!

An Iraqi official in plain clothes, accompanied by an assistant and a soldier, made his way over to our gathering. By his demeanor, I assumed he was Iraqi Secret Police. In the past, I'd had dealings with them and could recognize the profile. My sweaty palms were confirming this suspicion. He asked for everyone's passports, which we dutifully turned over. This man was all business and knew exactly what he was after. He was the man I feared all along; a person who, if anyone could, would know what Lee had been doing during our stay. Lee and I dared glance at each other. He hassled Dana a bit to no avail. He opened Dick's passport and instantly found what he was looking for.

"You have no exit visa," he authoritatively stated.

Dick offered a lame excuse, but knew he'd been caught. The officials in the visa office had somehow overlooked this and gave him permission to leave.

The Iraqi motioned him to be led away. Jane began to cry. Pat, to his credit, tried to intervene and was told to shut up, firmly. He complied without hesitation.

The Iraqi began scanning my passport. He gazed up from the document and barked, "You come with me!"

My heart shot to my throat and I thought my stomach would purge what little content was in it. I'm going to die I thought; I'm not going to make it after all. The needless, stupid delay was going to cost me my life. The Iraqi grabbed me by the back of my collar with pistol drawn from holster and led me back towards the customs hall. The others had become stone figurines.

I could just about walk as fast as he was dragging me. By now, I had become so mentally weary by the events of the last week that I just wanted this ordeal to end and I did not care how. We went through the customs hall, made a quick left and walked toward the office where the whole process began.

"You stay here," he said and disappeared around the corner of the building into the dark with my passport in hand. I stood there motionless, smoking and wondering what could have gone wrong. It was an eternity. He finally reappeared; apparently preoccupied with some other detail when he noticed me standing in the exact same spot he left me in.

"You still here?" he asked most obviously upset with me.

"I don't have my passport," I said.

"Come with me," he commanded and grabbed my arm and led me into the visa office. The place was in the same state of chaos I had left it in earlier. He shouted loudly in Arabic and a sea of men parted down the middle, most looking at him in terror. He banged a fist on the glass and said something I did not understand and my passport slid out from underneath the slit in the glass. He slapped it in one of my hands and escorted me out into the warm night.

"They did not cancel your re-entry visa and your residence permit!" he said. Don't you just love red tape?

There was a short cut through an alley between buildings so one could avoid having to go through the customs hall.

"Can I go through there?" I asked him.

"You are free to go anywhere you like," he replied. I thanked him in Arabic.

He answered, "You are welcome," smiled and walked away.

I had made it! He used the word "free." I rounded the corner and cast a long look at my colleagues. They were huddled in a little group about one hundred yards away. I thought nothing could eclipse the nightmare of impending death. The exhilaration of life outshined it. I strode slowly and confidently toward freedom. As I got closer I saw they were expressionless. I looked at them all, broke into a wide grin and exclaimed, "Let's go home!"

We started jumping around and hugging each other. The victory, however, was bittersweet. The Iraqis' led Dick back. He took Jane aside and she began screaming, "No, no, no, I'm not leaving you!" I didn't need to ask what happened. He was being returned to Baghdad. She would not loosen her grip on him and Dick motioned to Tex. Tex took her screaming and kicking, folded her in half and stuffed her in the back seat of the car. Dick was led away by the authorities. We crammed in the cars putting drunken Kevin next to the window in case he puked. The cars pulled out of the back of the outpost on the road and headed the short distance to the last Iraqi checkpoint. After another document check and a search of the cars for stowaways, they lifted the long iron bar and we crossed the border. Over the cracking car radio came none other than Jimi Hendrix playing the "Star Spangled Banner" from Woodstock. It was the most ironic instance of my life! As we rode along I was able to focus on only one thought as I stared skyward into the star filled night. There was now no question in my mind that God did exist nor would I ever in my lifetime challenge it again!

CHAPTER 9

Beyond the Yellow Brick Road

Our desert train headed into the Jordanian moonlight across a mutually respected twenty-six-mile-wide "no man's land" separating the two countries. It would not be until we crossed this barren strip would we reach the actual Jordanian border. I was told Jordan was accepting anyone into the country who was fleeing Iraq without a passport or visa. The mood in our car was jubilant. I didn't care how long nor what the hassles were in reaching Amman. I didn't even care if I had to walk! The road condition was poor and it took much longer to reach the frontier than you would normally expect a twenty-six-mile drive to take. When we finally arrived at our destination, it was floodlit and much secured. It was also besieged with reporters. We pulled the car over and disembarked. Ahmed took the passports and went into the border control to get us the necessary travel documents required for it was still a long way to Amman and Jordan was on a war footing. We also needed to get out of Jordan now that we had made it this far. The reporters, most notably BBC radio, swarmed around us. I gave some brief statements and showed off my handful of bullet shells. They wanted to know where we'd been for they had heard some Americans were at Al-Rouashid attempting to get out of Iraq. After explaining as briefly as possible what had occurred, the BBC asked me if we'd seen a bus full of Brits at Al-Rouashid. It appeared they were overdue in Jordan by about two hours according to their original estimate. I said I'd seen no bus whatsoever of any nationality. Only later did I learn that the bus, which had arrived at Al-Rouashid within minutes of our departure, had been turned back to Baghdad. It seemed Saddam had done exactly what I'd calculated and feared from before we left which was to seal the borders in every direction. In effect, I was the last man out. I shut out the lights!

Another reporter told me I'd just missed Dan Rather, or "Gunga Dan" as he referred to himself as. He'd been waiting at the border for escapees for hours and finally gave up and drove back to Amman. With any luck, I thought, I could avoid him tomorrow. *Der Spiegel* asked me for a few words. Two freelance photographers working for *Stern* magazine asked me for photos of anything and that they would pay top dollar for them. I didn't have any. They'd all been destroyed earlier.

While Ahmed was inside processing our entry visas, I decided to have a chat with the reporter from the BBC. I told them who my father was and the empire he ran for many years in England. I appealed to him as an Anglophile to urge the BBC to stop broadcasting reports that missile and aircraft attacks by the United States on Baghdad would occur soon and without warning. These broadcasts were being monitored by the people still captive in Iraq by short-wave radio were not only adding to the misinformation and confusion, but were generally scaring the shit out of everyone. Further, these people were not being detained. Being "held against our will" was a polite, diplomatic form of government phraseology for what no government wanted to publicly admit. The fact that Saddam Hussein was holding the foreign population within his borders hostage and the sooner the world recognized and accepted this simple definition, the better off those being held were going to be. I was prepared to threaten anyone with information I had to achieve this objective. The reporter listened sympathetically and told me he'd relay this news to Athens where he was posted and they in turn could forward it to London. You could always depend on the British for civility.

We had spent considerable time at the border before all was in order to push off for the capital. It was a long, straight drive to Amman across the wasteland of the Jordanian frontier. There was considerable traffic in both directions. Primarily, trucks were heading

toward Iraq, cars away from it. We listened to the radio. We listened
to Kevin's drunken babble. I chain smoked Marlboro 100s. I talked to
Ahmed who sat next to me in the sagging front seat. He had worked
for Citibank all his life and was now Chief of Security for the branch
in Amman. From the looks of him he wasn't paid shit for this job as
was the case with Citibank no matter where you work for them. He
was married and a grandfather. His only son, an air force pilot, was
shot down and killed in the last war with Israel. Although the death
of his son was tragic and untimely, he bore no animosity towards the
Jews. Periodically, we ran into roadblocks. Young soldiers, barely old
enough to shave, would thrust machine guns into the windows of
the car and demand our passports. After a while, this was becoming
more routine than anything else. The Jordanians certainly appeared
more prepared for conflict than the Iraqis' did. There were tanks,
cannons and armored personnel carriers all along the route inbound.
We passed multiple convoys of them heading outbound. I tried to
sleep and couldn't, assuming I was beyond exhaustion and the nic-
otine wasn't helping any. The road seemed endless. Around 1:00 in
the morning, we pulled into a tiny, dimly-lit town, more of an oasis
than anything else. I was angry we were stopping but Ahmed told me
the drivers needed food and tea. We piled out of the cars and into a
roadside café. The drivers ate flat bread. Most of us were too tired or
sick to consume anything but the tea. I ventured outside to find the
bathroom. Upon entering, I discovered this one made the bathroom
in Al-Rouashid look like the recipient of the Mobil Five Star Award
for clean restrooms! I held my breath again, voided rapidly, and left.
As I was walking back to the café, Kevin came swaggering toward me.
The amount of time on the drive hadn't made much of a dent in the
level of his intoxication.

"Where's the shithouse?" he asked.

"Just over there, can't miss it," I replied.

"Is it clean?" he wanted to know.

"Why it's spotless!" I said trying to maintain a poker face.

Shortly after he entered, I heard the unmistakable sounds of his
guts retching up. The son of a bitch deserved it! I rejoined the group
and waited for the drivers to finish eating. While sitting at a long

table, I witnessed an interesting little procession. The proprietor of the café, a young man in his early twenties, walked outside carrying a small wooden table. He then returned and carried out three wooden stools. Then he came out with the largest hookah pipe I'd ever seen! It was easily three feet high with many pipes. The drivers finished eating, Ahmed paid the bill and it was time to complete this odyssey. As I walked outside, a faint but familiar aroma filled the air. I got closer to three men sitting around the table for a better look. There was no mistaking the sweet perfume of hashish. Ah, the memories flowed unabated. There sitting in the bowl of the pipe was a chunk of blond hash the size of a child's wooden alphabet block. I convinced myself this had been a grueling ordeal; I'd answered the call, rose to the occasion and was most deserved of a couple of tokes on that pipe. If not for anything, but for old time's sake!

As I approached the table to pick up the pipe that was being extended to me by one of the men, I felt a soft, gentle and wiser hand on the nape of my neck. I turned abruptly and looked at the smiling, fatherly face of Ahmed steering me away from the pipe and toward the waiting car. If he hadn't, I'd probably still be there today!

The hills and lights of Amman approached over the horizon. We wove our way through the sleeping city, being stopped intermittently by soldiers for yet more passport checks. Citibank had made reservations for us at the Marriott Hotel which when we arrived, resembled more of an armed fortress than a hotel. It was well past four something in the morning. The journey from start to finish, at least this portion of it, had taken sixteen hours. There were messages for everyone. Pat's ex-wife sent one that merely said "Congratulations!" I thought it was cold. I felt sad for him because I knew he still loved her deeply. Ahmed stood off to a corner by himself, head bowed. Everyone thanked him, but no one had their hands in their pockets. It was clear these cheap pricks thought he was "just doing his job." I walked over, thanked him and pressed my last, crisp one-hundred-dollar bill into his palm. He looked down and threw his arms around me. More kissing. I wish I'd had more left. I would have gladly given it to him. It most definitely would have been more complicated without him. We parted for life.

I went to my room and ordered a burger and a glass of milk. I placed a call with the hotel operator to America.

"Son?' I heard my father say.

"Dad," I replied trying to hold back the tears. "I am safe and in Jordan!"

It was now slightly after 5:00 a.m. In two hours I would have to wake up and execute the next leg of this junket. All I wanted to do was sleep for a thousand years. But nothing could have prepared me for what was to happen in the next twenty-four hours!

I was in reasonably good shape for only two hours sleep. It must have been the adrenalin. After a long shower and dressing, I ventured downstairs for a leisurely breakfast at poolside. I had loads of time and my colleagues were nowhere to be found. I truly didn't care if I ever saw them again. My peace did not last long. The media at large had managed to locate our whereabouts. In the middle of my eggs, I was approached by NBC news and requested to give a television interview. My interest was really in leaving, not talking to the press. They cajoled me to the point where I consented. By now Lee, Dana, and Pat had arrived on the scene, anxious at the prospect of appearing on national television. I'd had my fill of TV years before having completed a bachelor's degree in mass communications. NBC took forever to get hooked up. Time was starting to slip by. Luckily, the first thing I did after breakfast was to go down to the travel agent in the hotel and acquire my ticket from Amman to London so I was ready to go. The political situation in Jordan could only be described as tenuous at best since King Hussein in his infinite wisdom had decided to back Saddam. No one could predict the effect this would have on the stability of the capital, particularly the airport. My three colleagues had no tickets whatsoever.

Ed Rable, a foreign correspondent of long standing with NBC, was to conduct the interview. Since the technicians could not "crop" the shot, it was decided to do two interviews, one with Dana, Lee, and Pat and one with me separately which suited me just fine. The questions asked were of a general nature. What was the mood inside Baghdad, had we seen any offensive weapons, how we were treated in captivity, etc. The three of them succumbed to nerves and mostly talked over each other as I expected they would. As the session ended, I urged them to go get ticketed and avoid the journalists for fear of getting stuck in Amman. Rable conducted a lengthier session with me but as had been the case with the first broadcast, it was marred by technical difficulties, including a fly that landed right on the tip on my nose! I just swatted it away and kept talking without breaking stride. A friend of mine's eleven-year-old daughter saw this on TV in Hawaii and told her mother how it was the "coolest thing" that I remained so calm and just batted the pest away.

The time we had given NBC had put us considerably behind the schedule that I wanted to keep. I asked Rable if NBC had some clout locally and could do something to make the experience at the airport more tolerable. Since we had given graciously of our time it was the least they could do. Rable said he would look into it. I dashed off to my room to get my bag, fully prepared to leave, only to find Pat giving an interview to *USA Today* newspaper. None of them had gotten tickets and had discovered they now needed to go to the other side of Amman to do so as they needed to be purchased directly through the airline. There was now about an hour to make the plane.

"Pat, fuck this shit!" I said. "I told you to go take care of the tickets. I'm leaving!" and out I went, only to be stopped by the *New York Times* while waiting for a taxi. NBC had asked if I'd do a spot on the "Today" show, but at this rate I'd be lucky if nothing happened at the airport!

I knew they'd be pissed, but I left for the airport regardless. There were armored personnel carriers throughout the city but no one was being stopped randomly. They were definitely ready for something, but I'm certain they didn't know what.

The airport was calm and very secure. After producing my documents and tickets, I asked the reservations attendant if NBC had called about holding the plane for my three delayed colleagues. Royal Jordanian Airlines said that NBC had indeed called, but they were not holding the plane for anyone. At least Rable had been true to his word.

I arrived in the departure lounge as they began boarding the flight to London. Waiting until the last minute to see if my straggling friends made it, I finally climbed aboard. Taking my seat, I discovered that Sam, Dr. Tomasz's old partner, was in the seat next to me. As it turned out, Sam's final diplomatic foray had failed and along with Dr. Mike Saba, they made a run for it. Sam and Mike fared better than we, for Sam had attained a "safe passage" letter from an Iraqi official in Baghdad that translated read something like "hands off these guys!" While we were downstairs fighting for our freedom, they were on the second floor of the same building, drinking tea with an Iraqi commander who gave them a military escort in an armored column all the way back to the Jordanian border. Some guys have all the luck!

The engines were revved. The plane was full, but we were still at the gate. I could only guess what the delay was. After about fifteen minutes, down the aisle came Dana, Lee, and Pat. I would have preferred to go it alone to London. Pat walked up to me and called me a "Judas" and took his seat in the back of the plane. That was the thanks I got for saving his life!

It was a long, boring flight to London. Sam slept, I couldn't. My mind was far too exhilarated to be out of the Middle East completely for it to rest. For me, going to London was like going home, having gone to school there and living with my family for several years. I had told Pat to tell John in New York if we got through to book us in the Savoy Hotel. Shit, it was the least they could do to let us live it up for one night!

My bag came off the conveyor at Heathrow airport. As I walked out of customs, I got what I'd been expecting, a media circus. I walked all along past the arrival railing, flashbulbs popping as the press surged forward against the police. They encircled me, blurting out their questions, lunging microphones and cameras into my face. I gave them about five minutes in all when I noticed my teammates coming up behind me. But by then it was all over albeit a few token questions for them.

One question in particular, "Do you work for Mr. Norman?" infuriated Pat. By that time, I had spied a welcome sign, a man in a chauffeur's uniform accompanied by a young lady with a sign that read "Savoy." As I bullied my way through the throng, a correspondent from ITV grabbed me by the arm. Would I appear on their breakfast show in the morning and if so, could she come over to the hotel later for say, an hour or so of background? I reluctantly agreed.

I did not really fancy much more of the spotlight; however, I believed I could use my "fifteen minutes of fame" to do something positive. I was deeply disturbed and angered by the fact that our government and media were still referring to those being held in Iraq as "detained against their will." Saddam had already rounded up the foreigners there and moved most of them into the confines of the Al-Rasheed Hotel and selected a few unfortunates as "human shields." These people were not simply being detained. They had become a card, a bargaining chip to be used against the rapidly forming Allied coalition. They were in every sense of the word, hostages. Perhaps if I could make enough noise and cause our government sufficient embarrassment, I could effect a change in their status and what better way to do this than making an ass out of yourself on television!

Along the route to the hotel, I pointed out all the pubs I got drunk in during my youth, trying to revive some level of comradeship following my media coup. I had after all saved their lives. It was my courage, my plan, my money, and they knew it.

The Savoy, being an institution of irreproachable decorum and class, a true bastion of the British aristocracy and days past, was devoid of any press. After registering, I phoned my father who had been busy canceling other plane reservations and hotel bookings. Flights were made in as many directions as possible from Amman as well as multiple hotel bookings through European cities to throw off the scent of any potential terrorist reprisals against us. He had already alerted his security apparatus in London as to my arrival in fact, one had already delivered sterling in my name to the hotel. Dad, the consummate organization man if ever there was one!

It didn't take long for the ITV representative to show up. We spent one and a half hour's together civilly drinking tea in the lounge. I emphasized that I wanted to be asked questions pertaining to the status of the hostages. She agreed to pass this on to her producer. She also informed me a car would collect me at 6:00 in the morning to deliver me to the studio. *Uggh!* Still no sleep.

I adjourned to my room to make a few more calls and flipped on the TV. It was the dead of nightly news time. I couldn't believe it. I was all over every channel that had coverage at the airport! As I spoke on the phone, I soon became bored with the image of myself and switched on cartoons.

We had made dinner reservations at the stately and somber Grill Room in the Savoy, thinking it was wiser to remain close to the roost rather than venturing out about town. By the time I joined the gang, they had been in the bar drinking for an hour. They were well on their way and in no pain. The maître d' placed us in a banquette toward the back of the room where we'd be certain to bump into the backs of other diners along the way. After a short time, reporters began to appear in the lobby and gave notes to waiters to pass on to us and one or two of us would go out to see them. This began to disturb the ambience of the room as well as proving a minor irritation to some of the guests, particularly a Korean businessman and his well-heeled hooker. We became raucous and drunk, but really didn't care. After all, how often does a person go through such an ordeal? Since dinner was virtually complete, the maître d' suggested we move our act out to the bar, which we graciously complied with. Out in the lobby, several correspondents from the *Sun* tabloid had assembled. They took a few photos and inquired if we would go out on the town with them where we could provide a little "color" about our escapade. Tabloid journalists; how I detested them! Most reviling was the British with their de rigueur "tits and ass" photos on page two. I told Pat to go talk to them, gave him a hundred pounds, and off they trolloped. Lee and Dana returned to the bar. Me? I was going to bed. It was now, once again, one o'clock in the morning and I had to get up in four hours.

What there was of the night was brief. The ITV driver was as suspected, punctual to the minute. It was a bright, warm London morning, rare as it was, and I thought how wonderful it would be to have nothing better to do than to spend the day shopping. I was hastily introduced to the ITV staff that would administrate me during my brief tenure there and whisked me off to make-up. Following a brief powder, I was paraded to an antechamber where I was told to wait and watch the show. During one commercial break, they walked me onto the set, strung a mic around my neck and took a voice level check. I'd done a lot of "live" television and not much had changed in fifteen years, especially in broadcast news. They didn't even bother to introduce me to the co-hosts. I wouldn't be staying long enough for it to matter. ITV had arranged a remote "hook-up" with a young man whose brother I had briefly known in Baghdad. The family was terrified since they had lost touch with him. I knew the man in question had been moved to the Al-Rasheed Hotel and they needn't worry too much for he was presumably safe. The spot concluded, the floor manager unhooked me and I extended my hand in thanks to the hosts. They didn't even turn around. Outside, I told one of my handlers that if the family of the young man wanted to speak to me further, I'd be at the Savoy for a couple more hours. He seemed totally disinterested. They stuffed a check for fifty pounds in my pocket and carted me out the door. So much for humanity!

The driver had me back in the hotel by 8:00 a.m. I had breakfast and ran into Lee. He had been up all night, playing piano in some deserted banquet room of the Savoy and was still, beyond any undeniable fact, very drunk. His behavior was stranger than usual, very nervous, and extremely paranoid. I assumed the drugs and drink was beginning to take their toll. He said he wanted to stay in London for a few days; that he had friends here that he wanted to visit and who would look after him. I told him I thought it best he gets on a plane with me in a few hours, but he became insistent and belligerent. Having had my fill of his shit for many weeks culminating in the DIA debacle, I was less than in the mood to tolerate any more of it.

"Call Washington yourself and get their approval," I said. "I don't have the authority to give you permission especially with the condition you're in!"

I dragged him to my room, made him wash his hands and face and gave him a couple of Xanax, which he had returned to me, so he could sleep. He said it might take more than a few so I dumped most of what remained in the bottle into his trembling palm. While trying in vain to talk some sense into him, the telephone rang. It was CBS News in London, a Miss Deborah Thompson calling. Would I be willing to do a spot on CBS radio and then appear on "The CBS Morning Show" with Harry Smith and Paula Zahn?

"Uh, I don't think so," I said. "I've already done British TV, been up since five and I don't want to miss my flight home."

"Don't worry," she responded. "Our driver will pick you up, bring you here for the taping and then take you straight to Heathrow."

Again, I repeated that I wasn't interested.

"Aw, come on," she said. "You talked to the Brits. Give us a break and talk to our people."

She made me feel like a scumbag, so I relented. I said goodbye to Lee and again warned him I was not taking responsibility for his behavior nor expenses.

Well, here we go again! Alan, their driver, arrived precisely at 10:30 and it was off to CBS in Knightsbridge, not far from Harrods. CBS could not have been more hospitable and congratulatory. Deborah as`ked if there was anything CBS could do for me and I asked if they'd call my parents to tell them I'd be on television. I knew it would be a moment any parents would cherish as well as seeing firsthand for themselves that I was in one piece. They took me in to do radio. It was just a brief piece and remarked how calm I was for a novice. I told them I was no stranger to the process. I had hammered the issue of being hostages relentlessly and became pleased with myself that I had agreed to do this, as opposed to my experience earlier in the day. It was then time for the TV broadcast. Alan stayed with me the whole time, becoming a most consoling figure. They sat me on a stool in front of a window overlooking a busy thoroughfare; the window you usually see Robert Fenton, their senior correspondent, occasionally broadcasting from in front of. The floor manager ran a wire up my back and put a mic in my ear. The producer came on from New York and told me he'd heard I knew a thing or two about this business and that not much had changed since my day. The cliché was being overplayed. They would go to a commercial, count me down coming out of it from ten into Harry's introduction. I had no monitor; just stare straight ahead to the red live light on top of the camera. It was a breeze and great fun, like reliving a part of my past long since gone. CBS remarked about my professionalism. I was truly flattered. Harry Smith was courteous and polite, but I would have preferred Paula Zahn. I always thought she was a knockout! Or Mark McKuen? Ever notice how every national network morning show has a fat, black weatherman? Even after Willard Scott left the scene, along came Al Roker! The same type of comparison could be made for evening, regional news. They all have a token young, attractive oriental female newscaster in the Connie Chung mode. In either case, I've wondered why.

We wrapped it up, said our goodbyes and Alan drove me to the airport. Along the route, he told me some great CBS gossip. Dan Rather, whom I told Alan I just missed at the border in Jordan, was really a nice, obliging fellow. He once broke a newscast in front of Buckingham Palace to give a group of school children his autograph. I guess he couldn't be all that bad! After all, his wife did date Elvis. Maria Schriver was arrogant and talentless; a Kennedy true to form. It turned out that Forrest Sawyer had to carry her through the broadcasts or they'd never made it. *Hurray for Forrest*, I thought! He was a first-rate journalist who got the shaft by the network for being teamed up with Schriver and they lost the vicious ratings war for morning news shows. I'd heard most of the Kennedy offspring were not very bright, great to look at but rather dim. Maybe too much Irish inbreeding?

Inside the waiting lounge, I called my folks in the States. They had indeed seen the broadcast. WRAL, the local CBS affiliate in Raleigh, had awakened them at 6:30 a.m. to tell them I was going to be on television. After seeing me on TV, my four-year-old nephew said to my sister, "Gee, I didn't know Uncle knew Harry Smith!"

My father told me the local media was more heightened than previously as a result of my being on multiple news programs and several newspapers wanted to be told when I was coming home. Dad asked me what I wanted to do.

"Don't tell them a thing," I said. "I'd like to slip in as quietly as possible."

The following day, by sheer coincidence, my family was making their annual pilgrimage to the beach for two weeks. Emerald Isle, North Carolina is one of the most pristine and tranquil spots I know of and I'd be able to relax and be secluded with just my family.

Fuck 'em, I thought. *If they wanted me, they can come and get me!* I wish I'd known the irony of that statement when I made it.

Pat and I had an uneventful flight home. The plane was virtually empty which was a welcome advantage. Dana was flying direct to Boston and then to his home in Rhode Island. It was finally over.

But what had it been all about? Looking back at the events of the last year and piecing them together, any layman would have realized something momentous was going to occur, but we just couldn't figure out what. No one could.

During the eight-year war that Iraq fought with Iran, Kuwait had inched their border with Iraq up progressively while the fighting raged on. By the conclusion of the war, the "new" border had encroached one strategically significant piece of real estate. Now, greater Kuwait covered one-half of the Rumaillah oil field, one of the largest known to man. The portion they absorbed was also known to have the deepest reserves, leaving the Iraqis' with the short end of the dipstick, so to speak. Saddam appealed both to Washington and the United Nations for assistance but was turned a deaf ear. Yes, he was good value in terms of counter-balancing Iran's threats of Fundamental Islam spreading through the region. He and his army also provided a buffer to the soft, underbelly of predominantly Muslim Soviet Republics. They would have to traverse Iraq to reach their targets of expansionism. This is why massive arms infusions reached Iraq late in the eight-year war; the US needed to assure he would be victorious. If Saddam were defeated it would complicate the larger task at hand, dismantling Communism in the Soviet Union.

As any diplomat of experience will tell you US policy toward the Middle East could not be much worse. The reason the Palestinian crisis has been allowed to go on for twenty years is because we don't really give a shit in terms of a permanent resolution. It is not strategically, politically, or economically important. Subsequently, when Saddam rang the White House doorbell, believing he was due his fair share for having fought this eight-year tragedy costing a generation of men on behalf of Saudi Arabia and the US, he was told to fuck off. Only was this point proved than after Desert Storm when "Stormin' Norman," the other one than me, was seventy kilometers from Baghdad and Bush wouldn't allow him to go any farther and bring down this despot. For Saddam was now required to serve the same purpose as previously explained, as a deterrent. He was, once again, strategic to our interest in the region. So what if he went on to slaughter Shiites in the south and Kurds in the north; let alone countless thousands in Baghdad who were guilty of nothing? Our government's need for his services prevented trying Saddam for war crimes, or crimes against humanity, in the World Court in The Hague. Anyone who has ever had the experience of seeing firsthand pictures of Kurds he gassed, or had a friend tortured find this policy unbelievable; a crime more monstrous in proportion than Saddam himself. Saddam is far easier to rationalize and understand if you take him at face value for what he really is a gangster and his Baathist thugs and stooges. Ditto Hafez al-Assad in Syria. As Tariq Aziz reflected, "We've been in power too long."

James Baker was partially correct which took him forever to admit to the American people. Yes, this was about oil. But it was also about the reelection of George Bush, which I will discuss later. If Bosnia had oil, we'd have been there in a heartbeat. But they were nothing but poor, lowly Muslims, so who gives a shit? As the late President Richard Nixon stated, "If they were Christians or Jews, we probably would have done something about it." But you have to "pay to play," so no oil, no salvation. This is, in general, why we Americans treat Arabs with such contempt; they are expendable. If not for oil, we would more than likely let them annihilate one another, have the Israelis do it, or do it ourselves in some kind of global move against a Pan-Arabic vision of the sort Nasser was attempting to build. Kuwait historically was the nineteenth protectorate of Iraq before the British painted lines in the sand and installed kings. Saddam's bankroll was depleted more severely than most realized, and not getting neither economic nor political assistance from the global body. He did the most logical thing any thief with the military might he possessed would do. He stole it! I once asked a Bechtel engineer working on the refinery in Basra what would happen if the world lost one major oil-producing country like Kuwait?

"Not really very much," he replied.

"Why not?" I asked.

"Hell, we'd do something we've been asked to do for the past five years and haven't had the time or available resources to do," he said.

"What's that?" I inquired.

"Why put so many holes in Russia that it would look like Swiss cheese."

Liberate Kuwait? My ass! Democracy? I don't think so. Kuwaitis will be held in the same form of human and spiritual bondage as the Saudis' until the end of time. It is what those with money and power are allowed to do.

History itself also provides an interesting perspective into the psyche of Saddam Hussein. The cornerstone of the Al-Rasheed Hotel reads, "Constructed in the era of Saddam Hussein." Not the "term" nor "presidency," but *era*. Saddam had almost a religious-like devotion to the ancient ruler, Nebuchadnezzar, a king of king's in a period of Mesopotamia's past glory. He saw himself as the modern-day version of Nebuchadnezzar; expanding his borders into what his inner circle called "Greater Iraq." The Israelis' claim he had a coin minted with this map on it which naturally included Israel itself. So obsessed with this past ruler that he was that he had a chamber in one of his fortresses' filled with artifacts of priceless value in which he would pay homage to the great ruler. It's sort of like Madonna's infatuation with Marilyn Monroe, except on a grander scale. He was to manifest this vision with the expansion of Iraq. The planned reconstruction of Babylon also bore this out. Although he was technically elected President, Saddam was always addressed and referred to as "His Excellency." Large photographs of him in every fashion of dress but pantyhose adorned the Baghdad streets. This is not unusual for Arab rulers, despots, and dictators. It was rumored Saddam took it one step further; a photo of him must be hung on every wall at a distance of no greater that ten feet apart! Personality cult? No, he had transgressed organized religion where man becomes God himself. Scary concept? Just talk to the followers of L. Ron Hubbard and you'll see just how real this can be even in of all places America!

There even exists a more plausible analogy. In the "myth" of Saddam Hussein, as a young Baathist party member, he was shot in the leg while trying to escape a botched assassination attempt on the former king. On route to safety in Egypt, he dug the bullet out with his fingers. Once in Cairo, he was sheltered and became a disciple of one of the greatest of all zealot rulers, Gamel Abdel Nasser. They became like father and son and through Nasser, young Saddam learned the tricks of the trade, or "how to seize power for the alleged welfare of the nation and stay in it a long, goddamned time!"

Nasser's dream was Pan-Arabism, a twenty-two-nation conglomeration stretching across the sands of North Africa, into black Arab Africa, all the way to the eastern end of Persia. Of course, what better choice of ruler for this maniacal empire than, you guessed it, Nasser himself! It didn't fly. Arabs are tribal in birth, as well as in custom and nature. They can no longer get along with each other than they can with the Jews. And they've had two thousand years of practice at that and they still can't get the hang of it! This is what Saddam saw when he brought the leaders of the Arab world together for a three-day blowout in Baghdad. The manifestation of Nasser's dream; something greater in proportion than the Arab Maghreb Union. Pan-Arabia with Saddam himself enshrined as king! And Baker said this was about jobs?

Our plane lumbered into Dulles. I had very little time to make the connecting puddle jumper to Raleigh. Waiting outside the gate were my travel agent Cathy Wilcox and her husband Dick. Cathy and Dick had labored through the previous night making all the bogus flight and hotel reservations to throw any would be assassins off course. Also, there was my old college buddy, Fred, who lived in the area. No family came to meet Pat. I felt terribly sorry for him, for after such an ordeal as this all he could look forward to was an ugly divorce. Poor bastard! Not to be outdone, not a soul showed up to welcome us home from our firm. Our office in Georgetown wasn't even forty-five minutes away and not one of them had the professionalism nor decency to be there if nothing else but to say, "Welcome home, dickheads!" Amazing what the state of American business has degenerated into than better exemplified by the greed and arrogance of our firm. But the worst was yet to come.

Cathy commented we better get on our way as she had spied a horde of reporters from CNN, presumably looking for Pat and me.

I arrived in Raleigh as I had left, in darkness. It was as quiet as I had hoped. My parents ran toward me and I fought to gulp back the tears. My mother, being Italian, was her usual overemotional self. My father, being of German extraction, was a study in composure.

Our reunion at home did not go undisturbed for long. Within ten minutes, the phone rang. It was Lee calling from London. He was drunk, either again or still, and seemed in a state of total paranoia. He said he had information that Iraqi agents were going to kill him and come after me in the States, allegedly for derogatory comments I made to the press in reference to the situation, as it existed in Iraq. I asked him what proof he had and his response was it wasn't safe to discuss this on the phone. It was not a secure position to assume he was bluffing or deranged. He had inferred that very possibly the DIA information had leaked after all. Lee was so frightened he had alerted British authorities that in turn mobilized an antiterrorist unit. I pleaded with him to get out of the Savoy, but he was adamant that he was at less risk in the hotel than out. Saying I have a plan, I agreed to call him back in two hours. I wasn't terribly worried about our safety. Foreign agents have great difficulty operating abroad because there is no internal support infrastructure here in the States. My father purposely would not allow reporters from the local papers interviews because he did not want photographs of our family or residence published. I woke up Cathy and told her to go to her office and make fifteen plane reservations in any direction emanating from London in Lee's name. Only one of those bookings should be confirmed to Copenhagen. Then I called an old family friend in Denmark and explained the situation and asked him to stash Lee for two weeks until we could quietly arrange to get him back into the States. Claus agreed, as I knew he would. I then called Lee back, told him the plan, gave him the one confirmed flight itinerary and Claus's telephone number.

I finally made it into my own bed. As I lay there, feeling the soft mattress with the palms of my hands, I recalled my thoughts in Baghdad when I believed I would never sleep in this bed again. Of the 586 foreigners taken prisoner by Saddam Hussein, only 11 of us escaped. The statistics were appalling and a true condemnation of allied diplomacy in the face of the enemy. However, in light of what had just transpired in the last forty-eight hours, it remained remarkable to me how one could go from unquestionably the worse day of your life to the greatest day of your life literally overnight!

I awoke to sunshine, woodpeckers, and my mother's radiant smile. Before leaving for the beach, I decided to check with Claus in Denmark to see if Lee made it. Claus never heard a thing. It was now out of my control as well as my hands.

Sitting alone in the back seat of my father's car for the three-hour ride to the shore, I listened to Joni Mitchell's "Court and Spark" on my Sony Walkman. Some twenty years later, it was still a deeply moving and timeless masterpiece. Every time I heard it, the album always took on a new meaning. For some reason, thinking about the past week, I felt very alone and angry that someone had indeed tried to kill me; a violation of sorts. I began to weep. It was the first time in a very long time that I cried for myself. Perhaps, it was just the pain of the past merging with the uncertainty of the future.

My father had rolled the phone over from our house in Raleigh to the place at the beach. In the process of unpacking the car, it began ringing off the hook with requests for exclusives and interviews. Remember my earlier declaration about coming to me if they want me? Well, they did, by every means of transportation conceivable! Deciding to keep the horde away from the house, I decided to hold court at the local Sheraton hotel about a mile down the road. The hotel was most cooperative about the disturbance to the guests but had a fit when the helicopter from WRAL-TV tried to land in the parking lot and almost tore down the power lines! I gave interviews to every major network affiliate in either the pool area or the fishing pier behind the hotel. The vacationers adapted to a carnival-like atmosphere to the proceedings. At times it became a bit bizarre with one network asking me to wade ashore in camouflage pants, bandana around my head, and bullet bandolier wrapped around my chest. When I tried to explain that the only ocean reaching Iraq's shores were nowhere near landlocked Baghdad and the Persian Gulf did not have four foot breakers, they were reluctant to believe me. It more or less confirmed my suspicions that most media types never graduated from high school. A public relations firm called and wanted to represent me. They said I had become the hottest news story in America in the last forty-eight hours. Radio stations in Phoenix, where for some reason the story became very huge, had me doing "plugs" or commercials over the phone. For the most part, I kept pushing the "detainee vs. hostage" issue; the only real reason I was subjecting myself to this circus. The press was accurately carrying my message. Only a few papers went the tabloid route. *North Carolina Business Weekly* magazine referred to me as the real "Indiana Jones." It's so comical to read about the things you didn't say and the things you didn't do!

My finest piece was an interview with Inside Edition, long before they turned into tabloid trash. I spoke to them for over an hour in an unused banquet room of the hotel. Much of the material was information not previously released. My father kept interrupting the taping, questioning issues he believed concerned national security. He had become my de facto press manager. Following the taping, they had me walk several times up and down the length of the pier with suit jacket draped over my shoulder. The only thing missing was Frank Sinatra! They had me pose for long gazes out over the Atlantic coast. Corny was not the word for it. Of the hours of tape, they used only seven minutes!

This carried on for three days. I gave an interview to *Time* magazine. The Governor's office called requesting my address. My father wanted to know the reason, as he answered the phone. When told they didn't know, that the request came from the Governor himself, my father hung up on them.

"It may cause problems on your tax return," he said. Why? I couldn't figure out. The Governor probably wanted to give me a citation of merit or a medal, that's all!

Oprah's people called. She wanted to fly me to Chicago for a taping of her show along with a volleyball instructor who escaped from Kuwait. Dad told her producer we weren't interested. The producer shot back with the fact that they knew twenty million Americans who watched Oprah daily. Dad said, "We don't care!" and when the producer started screaming, my father hung up the phone on him. I knew then why Michael Jackson fired his own father!

I didn't have any regrets missing Oprah. The "moral rot" she, and the likes of Geraldo, Sally Jessy, and Jerry Springer, purveyed are doing more to degenerate whatever family values and decency we have left in this country. They have, for the most part, turned the misfortunes of the down and out, into entertainment to the delight of many.

Through it all, I focused internally on my gratitude to God for being alive. I still found it hard to accept the fact that I haven't been killed. As I sat on the porch one afternoon thinking about this, my family crowded around the TV but I couldn't hear it because the glass sliding doors were shut. I could only see them through the glass huddled around the TV set. My father rose, walked toward the kitchen where the phone was, then returned and opened the doors.

"The President's on," he said.

"Oh my God! George Bush himself. What am I going to say to him?"

I collected myself a moment and went in to take the call.

"Okay, where's the phone?" I asked.

"Why?" Dad asked.

"The President? You know, the call."

"He's not on the phone, you idiot. He's on the TV!"

At this point, I thought this shit was beginning to get the better part of me. After returning to Raleigh, I agreed to one last program. It was to be a remote hookup from Raleigh into Fayetteville, or "Fayette-Nam" as it was known locally from the huge military contingent there. It had been a staging ground for many of our troops going over to fight the Vietnam war. The broadcast was to be a debate or town hall meeting between the Iraqi ambassador to the United Nations (a friend of Dr. Tomasz), some military types, a defense analyst, and a State Department representative. Because I was not in Fayetteville on the panel, I only participated in a minor way, trading a few barbs with the Iraqi ambassador. The lone cameraman in the studio with me appeared more bored than anything else. Perhaps he was right. I was no longer newsworthy. The country, and the world for that matter, was being set for a much larger show. The curtain was about to raise on the mother of all battles—Desert Storm!

CHAPTER 10

The Magic Kingdom

Before I left the coast of North Carolina, I had the opportunity to witness the staging of Operation Desert Shield. Tanks, missiles, planes, Humbvees, and troops were being dispatched to Morehead City, where they were bundled onto transports bound for Saudi Arabia. As I stood there watching this amazing mass mobilization, I couldn't help but wonder what all of this hardware and manpower was really going to be used for. Depending on your point of view, it was either going to engage and destroy the world's fourth largest army and a country of innocent people in the mother-of-all-fiascos, or guarantee George Bush's reelection. Were we going to engage Saddam for the sake of democracy? I don't believe you could have convinced any American of reasonable intelligence that this was true. Jobs according to Jim Baker? Again, the same answer. As Mayada once said to me in the days prior to the escape, "You can do whatever you want to us, but we've got your precious oil!" Bingo, you win! Now with that established, let's take a closer look at the Iraqi army.

I saw firsthand how this army was built. The "call to arms," or recruitment program consisted of rounding up able and often disabled Iran war veterans, herding them into huge dump trucks, and driving them, still in their street attire, into the desert. A Kalashnikov machine gun in your car window aimed at your head provided all the incentive you needed to sign up for the campaign. Daily, draftees careened through the Baghdad streets. During the eight-year war with Iran, Iraqi soldiers were provided with plastic keys to tape to their foreheads before being sent into suicide charges, attacking the Iranians in waves head-on. The purpose of the key was to "unlock the gates of heaven," if that was you final destination! Not exactly what I'd call a "well-honed military machine." These poor souls were slaughtered by the hundreds of thousands or worse, maimed for the remainder of their already hopeless lives under Saddam's regime. One of the final battles claimed in excess of fifty thousand lives; almost as many lives as the three days at Gettysburg. Sources informed me when the Iraqis' first received Exocet missiles; it took them twenty-seven attempts before they were able to fire one accurately, at one million dollars a shot! A simple yet useful analogy of their organizational capability, tactical, as well as deployable could be illustrated simply. Order a cup of coffee in an Iraqi hotel. The waiter would return in twenty minutes with a cup of tea! They ran out of Pepsi. When will you get more in? Tomorrow they said. It came in two weeks later. They ran out of red wine (bad "dago red" at one hundred dollars a bottle). Same question, same answer. It came in four months later! The Meridian Hotel under Iraqi management was never the same again. The list went on and on. This is a perfect reflection of ability versus reality.

When Desert Storm got into full swing and Iraqi soldiers were beginning to surrender, I sat with my father watching the CNN coverage. On the screen appeared the image of an Iraqi soldier; an old man with a rag wrapped around his head, black street shoes with no laces on the wrong feet with a dilapidated carbine he was using more as a walking stick than a weapon. You needn't look any further for an explanation than that as to their fighting capability for this picture said it all!

Only forty-five thousand soldiers of this million-man army were allegedly professionally trained members of the Islamic Revolutionary Guard Corps, an elite personal bodyguard for Saddam himself. And that is what we assembled the largest armada of men and machines since the World War II to fight against. It was a joke!

The war wasn't about oil or democracy; it was about politics, as most things in life are about one way or another. Bush had routed

Manny Noriega, one-time US employee turned bad in nothing more than a "police action." But this wasn't good or grand enough to insure reelection. The economy was in shambles and a racial explosion was simmering. Popularity was dropping fast. What's an incumbent president to do? To truly distinguish a good president from a great president, you need a war; a global, major, people-killing, rockets-flying, winnable, non-nuclear confrontation! A moral star-spangled banner, apple pie injected, "rally round the flag, boys" battle. Create more jobs by taking out your stored up toys of war and let the taxpayers see that all the bucks they shell out for this hardware is worth the price because this shit really does work after all! One of the best political cartoons I've ever seen was shortly before Lady Thatcher lost a vote of confidence in Parliament, which cost the general election. Maggie was kneeling in a prayer like position at the foot of her bed asking the good Lord to please send her another Falkland Islands War! George Bush never heard the bells of history tolling.

True, no modern air force has ever won a war single handedly. No, carpet-bombing doesn't work either. A "limited engagement" cost fifty-seven thousand American sons their lives in a shithole called Vietnam. Saddam moved his planes before the initial strike, for he knew the ground war was already lost. The psychological war from the Arab perspective was another story altogether. Any Arab nation, regardless of how large, wrong, oil or no oil, that stood up to America. and Israel did not lose face and made some kind of fight of it, despite certain defeat was a victory for all Arabs. This was even regardless of their global political and economic dependencies. Talk to the average Saudi. They act like we started the entire affair with our policies in Washington. They cannot understand why we the Americans, with all the natural resources in the Pan-Arabic region has to offer, treat them like dirt, and revere Israel as the fifty-first state. When you tell them elections, it doesn't add up. They don't understand the might, power, and money of the Jewish lobby in America and how it assured specific election results. The Israelis don't want peace because it's bad for business. You could pit father against son in the American Civil War, but Arab fighting Arab was different matter altogether. It was a question of shame.

Why didn't they ask us about our experiences in Iraq when we returned to Washington after the escape? Why would Washington trash dynamic business opportunities in Baghdad with mega billions already invested by some of the largest companies in the United States? Because they did not want to know the answers and didn't give a damn about the future with the presidential election in doubt. The Bush administration had slipped so badly that they didn't just need this war to distinguish Bush as a great president; they *needed* it to secure his reelection and save the White House for another four years until Jim Baker was ready to take the mantle. At the conclusion of the campaign, Bush's popularity approval rating soared to eighty-five percent. Heading into the election campaign, it peaked at ninety-one percent. Desert Storm delivered exactly what it was designed to do. What went wrong?

Saddam, at our insistence and with Allied support, remained in power as insurance against outbreak of a civil war in Iraq, which could have opened the door for a Soviet takeover. He went on to slaughter thousands more in the mountains to the north and the marshes to the south. The UN embargo? Arabs are born traders and thieves. It is in their nature like the nerve in your funny bone. They can't help but behave the way they do. The "Great Chameleon," King Hussein of Jordan, insured Saddam privately that the frontier and the overland route to the Suez and Amman would remain open. Saddam rebuilt his nation in record time to the point where the damage from the war was negligible and mostly transparent. And more important than anything else, Saddam retained his power, dignity, and reverence amongst his people for standing up to the "Great Satan."

I returned to Washington after a two-week hiatus only to find more bad news waiting. Lee finally staggered home from London and submitted an invoice for his expenses totaling $18,000! The senior partners were livid and in keeping with the fraternity of the partnership, blamed me for it. All along I knew they would, for that is how the system works.

I contacted Dr. Russell Smith. He was as cold as ice, like he didn't know me and didn't want to. I surmised his intentions were never to speak to me again in this lifetime and he didn't.

My boss asked me if I needed psychological counseling, you know, "hostage deprogramming." I assumed as long as I wasn't sitting in a closet babbling and drooling like some cretin, I was all right. This assessment was made hastily and premature, long before the nightmares set in. A British gentleman, whose name I recognized from the newspapers who was used as a "human shield," blew his brains out in his barn some months later in the tranquility of the Cornish countryside. My dear friend Tony was forced to remain in Baghdad due to pre-existing contractual conditions; to run the defense systems for the duration of the war. Those conditions were enforced, not due to Tony's dedication to his work, they were enforced by putting a gun to his head. He was tortured for his efforts and I don't believe he will ever be the same again, which is an understatement on my part.

I asked about my bonus. "Oh, you mean the ten percent I offered you," my boss said.

"No," I replied. "I mean the twenty-five percent of my gross that you promised me for managing this job before I accepted the assignment."

"Well," he began. "Things have not gone so well for the firm this year and you'll be lucky to get anything at all, let alone ten percent."

I remained calm and told him I was prepared to take my case up the corporate ladder to New York if needed. He warned me not to do it, but that he wouldn't stop me.

For in my absence, another development had unfolded. In addition to submitting twenty-two bids on consulting engagements globally and having all of them fail, three of my colleagues, one a dear friend, were being accused of stealing an existing opportunity and bidding it on their own as a separate company. It was to be a continuation of work for a Turkish bank in its second year of a modernization project in conjunction with a leading Florida-based software vendor. It seems an unwitting secretary stumbled across their proposal in a file on a computer. She became suspicious, printed it out and turned it in to "Mr. Do-Gooder" Ed, the senior partner in charge. Ed alerted corporate in New York and the shit hit the fan! Ex-FBI agents, now hired guns, came in with the local law enforcement and sealed up suspect offices with a yellow crime scene tape, seized documents and cassettes, purveyed a sense of total damnation around the Washington office. The "Gang of Four" denied any wrongdoing and was placed on an administrative leave, pending a full-scale investigation, and potentially leading to criminal charges being filed. Yes, they were as guilty as sin for they "owned" the relationship with the bank in question. The plot also included my boss, hence the four of them. The bank had accused one of them and the Turkish government of ripping them off to the tune of forty-seven million dollars they paid for support and a Florida-based software system. The Turks believe they had stashed some of the money away for later use involved. I often wondered where four of them were able to acquire the funds to open their own consulting company shortly after their dismissal from the firm. The incident made front-page news in the Turkish newspapers and has threatened US-Turkish relations but has been purposely kept at a low profile. No one in the scandal was ever prosecuted but most definitely should have been.

All of this resulted in New York deciding to close our offices in Washington, DC. They apparently had enough of our global antics despite the revenue we were generating. The "Gang of Four" was fired immediately as I mentioned earlier and the remainder of us was put on notice to find another job within the firm or get out. Ed told me not to take it personally. Ed retired on a big, fat pension, culminating a seventeen-year career with the firm of doing absolutely nothing but developing his personal real estate portfolio. As I searched my mind as to why this was happening to me, I felt ostracized; like I was to blame for losing the Rasheed Bank contract and returning in defeat. It was as if I had lost the war and lost "face" on behalf of the firm. One positive result was I gained a whole new understanding and respect for all those that served in Vietnam and how our country has mistreated them since the war's conclusion. In the long run, it's probably better to be a dead hero than one who comes home alive.

But what about my bonus? I told my boss to get me a meeting with Bob, the executive in charge of the International Consulting Division in New York. Following the escape, Bob sent each of us involved the identical congratulatory letter, stating, "He guessed he owed me a lunch" the next time I was in New York. Big fucking deal! I still wanted my pound of flesh.

Bob was a first-class nerd. He kept me waiting in his office for over an hour. I began by explaining my boss's offer of twenty-five percent of my gross salary as an "incentive" for managing the engagement in Iraq. Bob shot back offering his understanding that it was to be ten percent and added if I could produce a letter proving this, then there would be no argument as to what exactly I was owed. Of course, there was no letter! If there was a letter, they'd have to pay me the bonus and they never had any intention of paying me to begin with, which is why I asked my boss for a letter defining the terms that I knew he wouldn't write. Bob laughed in my face; he knew I could validate an offer was extended but could not confirm the amount without any documented proof. Other officers of the company could confirm an offer was made, but it would only serve as a verbal confirmation, which could be contested. Bob then tried another tactic. He told me no manager in the entire global organization was receiving a bonus of any amount for this past financial year. Bob himself was being relegated to a do-nothing job as head of our Towson, Maryland, practice as a reward for this year's non-performance. Bob wanted me to know if this was the firm's policy regarding bonus awards for the year, then why should he pay me a single dime? I told him above and beyond what was promised, that no other officer of the firm except Pat, and he only made periodic visits to Baghdad, had laid his life on the line for the glory of working for this firm. The contract had also netted an enormous profit as a result of my leadership. But more important than anything else was that the bonus was promised to me. Remember that word, promise?

Since these men lacked any morals or ethics altogether, I certainly did not believe for a minute my impassioned plea would serve any purpose. I thought of going over Bob's head, but his boss was a bigger dickhead than he was! I thought of going to the *New York Times*. I considered slipping a condom in Bob's raincoat pocket with a lipstick note reading, "if it was good for you let's do it again!" hoping his wife emptied out his pockets as most suspicious wives do. I thought of giving up for if this was the thanks you get for almost coughing up your life, maybe it just wasn't worth fighting for. If I ever had a doubt as to the value of my life and my loyalty to the firm, I didn't any longer. Never was I so disillusioned in my entire career. We successfully managed to void any degree of integrity in American business and reduced it to one operative word: *Greed!*

Eventually I received a check for six percent of my gross, minus every tax known to mankind. I then began the arduous task of searching for a new job. This culminated in two offers from the same partner in Bahrain. One was to live in Kuwait and assist them in reviving the shattered operations of Kuwait's looted banks. The second was to be the Director of the banking practice for the Middle East based in the "fun and sun" capital of the region, Riyadh, Saudi Arabia. It was likened to a choice between syphilis and the clap! If I was going to subject myself to returning to what now became my designated area of expertise, I was going to do it for big bucks and not the peanuts the firm paid me. I turned the offers down and took leave of the company. Months later I met Paul, the partner, at the Arab National Bank where the firm's Saudi affiliate was and had wormed their way into an assignment. He was a real "wanker." Paul asked me in hindsight did I think I made the right decision in not accepting his offers. I thought to myself "after meeting an asshole as big as he was, I was more certain of it now than ever!"

If the skies over Baghdad were illuminated, to borrow a now famous line from a CNN broadcast by Peter Arnett during Desert Storm, then someone had shut out the lights over Saudi Arabia. I flew into Riyadh in May of 1991, some two months after the conclusion of the campaign. It was to be my first contract as an independent in association with my old friends from Dublin, Kindle Software. The bank we were going to "modernize" was the Arab National Bank (ANB). At 120 branches throughout the Kingdom, it was by far one of the largest banks in the country. It was jointly-owned and controlled by one Sheik Rasheed (no relation to the Iraqi bank of the same name) and the Palestine Liberation Organization (PLO).

I awoke the first morning to look out the window of the Riyadh Palace Hotel to find the skies overcast. This is unusual in Saudi I thought for it very rarely rains and if at all, only in the winter. These skies were not your usual cloud covered color. They were a murky brown. Later, I learned this was a result of the oil well fires still burning unchecked in Kuwait. It was not until the afternoon when the wind picked up that the oil haze was blown further out into the desert. Breathing was like sucking on an exhaust pipe! Adding to the environment was the endless stream of AWACS and C-130's coming and going. I sincerely hoped that Red Adair could work a little faster to contain the blazes!

Riyadh, from a cosmetic point of view only, resembled Los Angeles. Its buildings are of the most futuristic design, primarily constructed of glass sheets and tons of chrome. The new Ministry of the Interior building is an inverted pyramid that resembles a spaceship in Star Trek. Riyadh's boulevards are wide and spotless, lined with the names of most of the top hotel chains in the world. The traffic is murderous but the highways are excellent. The city contains an abundance of restaurants offering most any cuisine imaginable, most of it excellent quality. Eating after all was one of the few legal forms of entertainment that exist. One of the other's is hanging out at the local Safeway supermarket, a kind of singles' dance for expats. Riyadh quite simply must be one of the few places in the world where it is against the law to have fun. There is not a fucking thing to do but work and that is primarily done by foreigners. Work, to the average Saudi, is anathema. A foreigner once asked a Saudi is sex work or fun. The Saudi replied, "It must be fun for if it was work, we'd have a Filipino do it!" There were three million people living in the Kingdom at that time. One million were Saudis; the rest were "guest workers." They did anything the Saudis' wouldn't do, which was mostly everything! The Saudis' sent their children to American universities like USC, or "University of Spoiled Children," where they bought a degree of choice and then returned to the Kingdom to sit on their asses and do nothing. For when you have more money than God, why bother working?

The "guest worker" population was comprised of mostly Filipinos and housed in larger compounds where they pretty much lived in the same squalor they were trying to escape from in Manila. They sent their entire salary home to their families. In Saudi, they were allowed to do nothing and go nowhere. To me, it was a heart-breaking example of human existence reduced to its lowest form. The Palestinians were another matter altogether. Since King Hussein backed the wrong horse in the war, their status in the Kingdom was now one of being in deep shit. I heard stories from Saudis of how Palestinians stood around radios and televisions, cheering at every denouncement made by Saddam or an Iraqi Scud missile was launched toward the Kingdom. Prior to the conflict, there was a plan afloat in Saudi to provide Palestinians with a type of legal residency status, like an "almost green card." This would entitle them to partic-ipate in the vast Saudi social services program. Depending on what circles you traveled in, some claim this transition would eventually culminate in a portion of the Kingdom itself, carved out of the desert as a Palestinian homeland, similar to how the Eastern European Jews carved out Israel from nothing and turned it into an oasis. After all, these were Arab brothers and since no one gave a shit about them, someone must finally do something or the problems were simply going to escalate and not go away as everyone just hoped they would. The Saudis would also foot the bill for running the place. It sounded to me like a global version of Manpower, Inc., the temporary staff-ing agency. Now the Palestinians were about to do "Exile on Main Street!" Instead of a new homeland, they were being rounded up systematically and deported to Jordan, since that was the country of origin for most of their visas. Not good career move for neither King Hussein nor Yasser Arafat!

The only other form of entertainment was shopping; shopping for a whole lot of shit you really didn't need. As long as the object was bright, loud and gaudy, the Saudis loved it! How many watches, gold chains, and boom boxes does a man need anyway? In Saudi, it's a national obsession.

Sex? I'm certain it existed someplace. One of the more common means was raping your Filipino maid. In Riyadh, one is reminded of the James Brown hit, "It's a Man's World." This is one reason the London to Riyadh flight is the most requested route of British Airways male flight attendants. Let's grease assholes and wrestle!

Women, when rarely seen, are covered from head to toe. For the most part, this should be considered a public service for in Saudi, everyone has moustaches.

Occasionally, I'd see a young Saudi couple out to dinner in a more fashionable restaurant. The wife was veiled and draped, including black lace gloves. If you looked discreetly and quick enough, you could catch a glimpse of a petite, snow-white ankle. These were the European girls who made the mistake of marrying Saudi wealth, only to discover they became prisoners in a gilded cage with the status of "significant receptacle." Most, if not all, Saudi marriages were arranged. Usually you married your first or second cousin. This inbreeding may account for the basic lack of intelligence of the average Saudi.

The religious police are all over the place. At night, they roam the 'burbs in Riyadh in Jeeps, listening for Western music with ladders at the ready prepared to climb over a wall to raid a party in progress, or so they thought. The ruling Saudis fear this Westernization more that the invading Iraqis. Recently in Jeddah on the Red Sea coast, young Saudi men have begun to resist the restrictions, citing the Koran does not require abstinence from liquor nor covering your woman from head to toe. These restrictions were created by the historical ruling family years ago to keep the mullahs happy and not interfering with the business of ruling. If fundamentalism took root, the House of Saud would fast be filing for unemployment and packing for Switzerland. The boys in Jeddah now pull up in their cars at traffic lights next to the religious police and shout obscenities at them and hit the gas pedal! The police give chase and the kids lead them down blind alleys while another group in the wait cuts off the exit. There, they beat the shit out to the police and leave them for half dead. Boys will be boys no matter what the country!

Riyadh sustained minimal damage during Desert Storm. The average Saudi would not have you believe that. The Saudis' will tell you how they rallied to defend the Kingdom, to protect women and children from their Arab brothers. At the first sign of trouble, most Saudis had shipped their families into the protection of the desert or Switzerland, whichever was handier at the time and hid under the bed whenever the air raid sirens wailed. Although they prefer to put on a macho, warrior-like appearance, most Arabs are devout cowards who would sell their granny for fear of their own lives. One scud hit the old section of Riyadh next to a highway overpass. The Saudis will take you to see this shortly after your arrival there as a matter of national pride. The "hit" should have been considered urban renewal for the corner it struck demolished a deserted, dilapidated old eyesore. With better aim, the Iraqis could have laid waste to the gold souk only a block away. American ex-pat's ran out to collect the scraps of the scud as souvenirs, which they proudly displayed on their mantles or created legends over it at cocktail parties back home. So they are not caught unable to defend themselves in the event Saddam plays a repeat engagement nor be "invaded" again by the unwelcome Americans, the Saudis have constructed one of the largest military airbases in the world, hidden down in the desert near the border with Yemen.

My partners for the ANB engagement were once again Dana and one Oliver D. Dana you already know about from our days in Baghdad. I recruited Dana to renovate the ANB's branches. He didn't begin until mid-summer. Oliver, who was the Chief Operating Officer, was semi-retired and living in Sarasota. He was a former Executive Vice President for National Westminster Bank in New York. Between him and me, we mutually knew about two hundred people in this business but we had never met. Oliver decided to do this job in Saudi Arabia because he thought it would be a "lark" of sorts for him and his family. They planned to split the income from his contract three ways, as sort of incentive for wife Phyllis and daughter Kerri to subject them to this ordeal. Kerri was going to buy a Porsche, Phyllis a motorized wheelchair since she suffered from multiple sclerosis and could not easily walk. I begged and pleaded with him not to bring them to Saudi; that this was a cruel and inhuman thing to do to women, let alone two that you loved. He didn't buy it saying that they'd be fine. I said they would never last. They didn't.

Oliver is one of the most unique people I ever had the privilege of meeting. He was the son of a German judge and Cuban mother who had escaped from Berlin at the close of World War II by spying for the Americans on the Soviets. His activities were used to buy their freedom and passage to Cuba with the help of the OSS, the predecessor agency to the present CIA. When Castro came to power, they fled. Oliver became a fervent anti-Castroist, agreeing to enlist as an informant for the FBI to infiltrate the Cuban exile community in New York City. One group he investigated was the Fair Play for Cuba Committee, whose one prominent member, Lee Harvey Oswald, when on to notoriety of a different kind. He did this until his cover was blown by a Texas newspaper while he was employed as a systems executive at American Airlines in Dallas. Oliver was a round, jovial man with a fondness for French pastry of which we could never pass the French bakery in Riyadh without Oliver's car pulling in for a brief nosh. I loved him to death.

Oliver was the type of profile who could dine with you, laugh with you, put his arm around you in true affection, pick up the tab and when the evening was over, put a bullet squarely in the middle of your forehead and walk away. His type were always the scariest, the most dangerous.

The ANB was managed by Eli Al-Haj, a Catholic Jesuit-educated Syrian who'd become an American citizen while studying in the United States. He was tall and handsome, immaculately groomed beyond the point of perfection. I also likened his personality to that of Adolf Eichmann. When he walked behind the stooping Sheik Rasheed with the Sheik's gold-braided robe dragging along the floor behind him, they resembled Emperor Palpatine and Darth Vader. In fact, that's what I called Eli behind his back, "Darth." His favorite pastime was smashing his telephone to pieces when he lost his temper. Eli liked to describe himself as "colorful." He also didn't know a microchip from a chocolate chip!

El-Haj lived in perpetual fear of the PLO power base that ran the bank from Amman. He had disposed of the Associate Managing Director who was also Sheik Rasheed's son-in-law and thought the guy was always plotting to take revenge on him thorough his cohorts in the PLO. Once opponents of Eli had concocted a plot accusing Eli of being a member of the Freemasons; considered an anti-Islamic cult in Saudi Arabia and punishable by death. Another time on a Friday, the only day of the workweek off, I came to the office only to find Eli hiding under his desk! The security guard downstairs failed to identify a "visitor" which was only me coming to see if Eli was in on his day off. Eli believed it was a PLO gunman was coming to kill him! At lunchtime on Thursday afternoon's, which was like "happy hour" on a Friday night, we would often have to dine together at one of the hotels as Eli's guests. Eli would offer us a ride, which we'd always try to decline unless forced to do so. When he'd climb in his black Mercedes and turn on the ignition switch, I'd put my fingers in my ears waiting for a bomb to explode! He was also the world's worst driver.

Oliver decided not to live in any of the compounds for foreigners which were still full of Allied military personnel, but out with John Q. Public, Saudi-style. He leased a villa with a huge pool and servant's quarters. His driver, Nazia, was once a chauffeur to Rajiv Gandhi. Nazia got his driver's license at Sears and never bathed. He was good bug repellent! Oliver went out and spent $80,000 dollars of the bank's money on furniture in two days plus a Lincoln Continental. Oliver purchased such useful items as an eight-foot pool table and an exercise treadmill. As fat as he was, I asked him what he was going to do with the treadmill, maybe lose some weight? We used it to pass pastries to him while he was shooting pool, sort of a horizontal dumb waiter!

Dana and I rented a house in a suburban neighborhood behind the World Bank, not far from Oliver's. It was a beautiful house complete with swimming pool, rose gardens, and a Filipino houseboy. He couldn't cook, shrunk our clothes in the laundry, and slept most of the time. We had a big Toyota Land Cruiser to get around in. It was well equipped with all the bells and whistle" we needed in the event we had to make a run for the border! I wanted to put two bumper stickers on the rear, "Honk if you love Palestine" and "Follow me to Israel," but Dana thought it was a bad idea. I felt like a prisoner in a golden cage, for all there was to do was work, read, sleep and the weekly run to the Safeway supermarket. I was basically miserable most of the time.

A brilliant young technician, Hathem Massad, introduced me to one of his school chums, Sheik Saeed Bawazir. They had attended the same technological institute in Saudi. Saeed owned a company called Atallah Systems, which primarily was in the network installation business. Atallah was the name of one of the former king's prize racehorses. Saeed was a soft-spoken, kind man who very badly wanted to do business with the ANB. They were a fledgling, start-up business trying to make a name for themselves in the Kingdom.

One evening, Saeed invited Haythem and me to dinner with his younger brother, an equally pleasant young man. The dinner started late and wore into the early morning hours. As the conversation dragged on, I became tired and itchy to go home to bed. A waiter came to the table and told Saeed he had an urgent phone call and Saeed excused himself to take it. Upon returning to the table, he looked somewhat upset and nervous.

"I have a favor to ask of you," he began.

"And what could that be," I replied.

"His Highness, Prince Bandar would like to meet with you," he said.

Looking puzzled, as this name was altogether unfamiliar to me, I asked him what relation did he have to the prince and why did he want to meet me, of all people.

"Prince Bandar is a schoolmate of me and Haythem's from the technology institute," he replied. "He is also a partner in Atallah Systems."

"Sure," I said. "I'd be delighted. Set it up and let me know what date and time."

"No," Saeed replied. "You don't understand. He wants to meet you right now!"

"Saeed, its one o'clock in the morning! I have to get to bed because I have to wake up early for Eli's 7:30 morning screaming session. Can't we arrange this for a more civilized hour, perhaps tomorrow?'

Saeed grew more nervous at my reply as it was most probably unexpected.

"Please, John," he pleaded. "This is very important. You just can't say no to a member of the royal Saudi household. It would be a great insult."

I knew there was no way out of this and agreed to go. Saeed looked greatly relieved. We left the restaurant, piled in some cars and off to the Prince's house we went for what I didn't know.

The Prince's house was modest by royal standards. It was not a castle nor a mansion, but rather a long, rambling ranch house of sorts, more resembling houses in Beverly Hills or Bel Air. Upon entering the driveway, the scene turned into an intense situation almost immediately. Well-armed guards approached the car from every direction. I almost shit myself! We got out slowly and when they recognized Haythem and Saeed, they relaxed their stance and lowered their weapons. Although this was well after Desert Storm, Saudi Arabia was still in a heightened state of awareness. We entered the house and were led into a room with no furniture except for a huge television set that was tuned into CNN. Around the room sitting on cushions were perhaps a dozen or so older men in robes. Haythem explained that these were the Prince's advisors. They sat there motionless and speechless. We took our places on some cushions and waited. And waited and waited. I was starting to get irritable as the hour was now growing late. Finally, accompanied by more advisors the Prince entered the room and we all stood up. Prince Bandar approached me and I didn't know whether to bow, shake his hand, or give him a high five. He was smiling, which put me at ease and most apologetic for his delay. He was a most cordial young man, in his late twenties, married, and a father. His grandfather was King Faisal. His father, Prince Khalid, was governor on one of the southern provinces, a man more interested in art and poetry than in politics and governing. Bandar was around eleventh in line to the throne.

He asked me about my background, my personal life, and how the work at the bank was progressing. Bandar wanted a contract for Atallah Systems at the ANB and assured me I would be looked upon favorably by him in return. My eyes lit up like a Christmas tree as visions of untold Saudi wealth danced through my head! Then the subject got around to the recent Gulf War. Politics was something I tried my best to avoid in all cases, but this time I wasn't going to get out of it that easy. The Prince was most dismayed at the impression purveyed by the Western media that the Kingdom was a helpless country who had to rely on others to defend it, particularly against its Arab brothers. He wanted to know why the Jews were looked upon so favorably by the United States while Arabs were scorned. I tried to explain it was a matter of elections and the fact that there was not much of a lobby in Washington to further the Arab cause and image amongst the American people. Bandar then started out on the Palestinians. Prior to the war, there was talk among the royal family of creating a Palestinian homeland in Saudi Arabia. In an effort to end centuries old discord between Jews and Arabs, the Saudis were considering carving out a piece of the Kingdom as I previously mentioned, proclaiming it a protected territory and offering Palestinians from all over the opportunity to live and work in peace. They would be issued national identity cards, passports and could cash in on the vast Saudi social welfare system that provided its residents medical benefits, insurance, housing, schooling, etc. It sounded to me to be a pretty good deal. That all went down the shitter when King Hussein of Jordan backed Saddam in the war and Palestinians in the Kingdom rallied around the wrong flag! Now the Saudis issued a general decree to expel as many of them from the Kingdom as fast as was humanly possible. Haythem winced and smiled this crooked, little grin as he is a Palestinian. The questions about the war dragged on and on. His views towards the Americans and how they "saved the day" were quite negative and ungrateful, which more than pissed me off, but I did nothing to let on. He told me zillions of dollars were being pumped into arming and training the Kingdom so this would never happen again.

An old man in a white room entered with a tray of tea. Bandar took one look at him, shook his head and put his face in his hands. The old man had a pistol stuck in the sash of his robe. The gun was so old that the casing was pitted and the barrel curved slightly to one side. The Prince explained to me the man was his personal bodyguard. He gave him the gun during the war when the old man complained about not being able to protect the Prince if he was attacked.

Never mind that the house was surrounded by enough troops to defend it against anyone! When the war ended, the Prince told him he didn't need the gun anymore but the man insisted on carrying it anyway. Bandar asked the man to hand him the gun. He cocked it open and removed a single bullet from the chamber. When I asked him why he had only one bullet, Bandar said that was all that was safe to give him!

With tea finished, the Prince declared the evening was concluded. He thanked me for coming and invited me to lunch with him the following Saturday. Bandar had been accepted to the International School of Business at Tuft's University and would be leaving Saudi Arabia for two years to complete his studies. So much for my visions of unending wealth!

That Saturday, Haytham and I returned to the Prince's house for lunch. The Prince was right on time for food was a priority. We marched into the dining room which had a long banquet table arranged. Joining us were about twenty-six of the Prince's advisors, mostly the same old men we had met previously, sans a few more. Bandar, his brother Prince Sultan, Haythem and I sat at one end of the table. Everyone else was seated more or less down range. The Prince had a funny little grin on his face and when I asked him what was up, he told me to be patient and I would soon see. In came the waiters with bowls of that great American lunch pastime, "Spaghetti O's!" I could just about contain my laughter. The advisors had never seen such food in their lives. They just stared at the bowls wondering how to eat this strange meal. One by one, they began putting the little pasta rings on their fingers and sliding them off in their mouths! The Princes, Haythem and I looked on in delight. These guys had red gravy all over their white robes by the time they had consumed their portions. This was all washed with glasses of liquid yogurt, more like drinking barium enema tracer fluid or white paint! I did all I could do not to heave my guts. More bank business, more anti-American sentiment. When we departed, I told Haytham I hope I didn't have to go through too many more sessions like these for they had lost their entertainment value altogether.

In mid-summer, Phyllis and Kerri had their fill of the "Magic Kingdom" and returned back to Florida. Oliver did nothing but worry which made the whole experience even more unpleasant than before. The more he worried, the more pastry he ate and the fatter he got.

By Thanksgiving, I was starting to crack under the strains of Eli's daily tirades, monotony, the sheer boredom and lack of sex. I decided to "volunteer" to go to Dublin to test a new piece of software that Kindle Systems had peddled to the bank. It was complete "vaporware," developed by Indian programmers with thick glasses, who worked for next to nothing for the Irish. The software was a piece of shit and kept blowing up daily. Cian, who sold the system to the ANB as well as to countless other Saudi banks, I nicknamed "Pinocchio." There was no end to what he would do to the Saudis to take money out of their pockets. My contract with Kindle ended in December and I had signed to go on as an independent for the month of January at twice the amount Kindle was paying me. The Irish claimed I had "gone native" and was not to be trusted. I didn't really care, all I wanted was to get this over with and get out of the Kingdom at any cost.

Kindle Systems was sold to ACT Systems for fifty million pounds! The guys who founded it became multi-millionaires overnight, including Cian. He promptly announced his resignation and moved to Bahrain to avoid Irish taxes. What a sport! The ANB kept asking me when I was going to come back to Saudi and I just kept stalling which made them very unhappy. A new man, Mohammed Al-Mansour, took over management of the project at the bank. I told Oliver the day I met Mohammed back in May that he was useless and he should fire him. Eli would have done anything we suggested at that point, as he was suspicious of everybody even his current wife. Oliver insisted he could "convert" Mohammed and made it his pet project. Oliver took the poor, mistreated Palestinians up as his cause and was constantly badgering the Saudis to pay them more money. This did nothing but upset the delicate balance between all nationalities that were forever in jeopardy of exploding. In some sick and twisted way, Oliver enjoyed terrorizing Eli and Mohammed throughout the contract. He was always befriending people in the bank that they couldn't stand and wanted to get rid of. Often I puzzled over what Oliver was really trying to accomplish.

I soon found out. Mohammed called me in Dublin and told me not to return to the Kingdom. Oliver and Dana were dismissed summarily. When I reminded Mohammed that the bank owed me the remainder of the contract, he said I could be assured that they would pay me. I was neither offended nor upset by this decision. All I could think about was getting back to my soon-to-b- wife and civilization in the States.

Oliver got out of the Kingdom with all of our money and shortly thereafter it was off to a land that was as much a sweet dream as Saudi Arabia was a nightmare for I had accepted a contract to work in Munich, Germany!

CHAPTER 11

The Truth About Gulf War Syndrome

If you are like me and at least seventy percent of all sane and reasonable Americans, you'd no sooner believe that Lee Harvey Oswald acted alone in assassinating President Kennedy than you believe in the Easter Bunny! How could we, as a nation, have bought off on such a bucket of shit? Eddie Fischer says that Lyndon Johnson did it. Well, that's all the proof that I need!

The truth about Gulf War Syndrome is not unlike the facts regarding the assassination, or for that matter, Agent Orange, or any other great myth that our government has twisted and distorted to serve its own purpose in the name of the American people. What they want you to believe is so far from the truth it is an insult to the voting public that we actually put these people in office as representatives and keepers of our laws, our conscience and our integrity!

Let me begin by first giving you a summary of what happened in the Gulf War. First, it is important to establish a background of information first then understanding the specifics will be easier in the long run. Certain facts and themes will be repeated as the story unfolds.

Thousands of American veterans were repeatedly exposed to low-levels of various chemical and nerve agents during the brief war. Few at the time suspected the real reasons for their temporary ailments, and those that did were ordered to say nothing. Many of these exposures occurred in consonance with alarms of chemical detection equipment, which higher authorities deliberately discredited and ignored. Health problems created by chemical exposure at the time were attributed to other causes—bad food, dry desert air, influenza, oil smoke, or atmospheric dust. The immediate exposure symptoms were always a combination of the following: burning of the skin, numbness of the lips, runny nose, blurry vision, difficulty in breathing, chest pain, vomiting, disorientation, skin blisters, memory difficulties, and fatigue with flu-like symptoms. Now the long-term symptoms are being seen. One hundred thousand of these veterans are sick and over ten thousand have died!

Several international studies have documented the long-term effects of repeated low-level exposure to modern military chemical and nerve agents. These effects are similar to those of Gulf War veterans. This has also been the experience among the Kurds of Iraq who today, are dying in large numbers. The Kurds symptoms include higher than normal incidents of cancers, mental and physical disabilities, increased occurrences of birth defects, higher rates of congenital miscarriages, and rising problems with infertility.

In the sixty days between mid-January to mid-March 1991, a half-million American veterans were amassed in the deserts of northern Saudi Arabia and Kuwait. Just north of them in occupied Kuwait and Iraq, were hundreds of Iraqi munitions storage bunkers with thirty-five thousand tons of chemical, nerve, and biological weapons. Almost all of these were blown up with American conventional explosives before, during and after Operation Desert Storm, and depending on the prevailing winds at the time; those in the area or downwind repeatedly received varying levels of exposure to these toxins.

The United States military's position until now has been that, "No chemical or nerve agents were ever released into the atmosphere by anyone before, during or after the Gulf War." This false statement has complicated medical attention for those with Gulf War Syndrome.

That the American people have not, until now, understood the reasons behind Gulf War Syndrome is because the Pentagon and senior military leaders deny that any chemical weapons or nerve and

JOHN NORMAN

biological agents were used or released during the Gulf War. This is a lie and they know it. Our veterans were repeatedly exposed for six weeks to low level "cocktails" of Iraqi chemical, nerve, and biological agents, not enough to seriously sicken them, but cumulatively enough to start the process. Exposure to chemical weapons, like exposure to radiation during an x-ray, is a cumulative poison. A lethal exposure in an hour will kill its victim just as surely as a lethal dose administered incrementally over two months.

At the conclusion of the World War I, thousands of American veterans gassed with mustard and lewisite in Europe were returned to the United States and discharged without government benefits. Most died early from a variety of cancers and associated illnesses brought about by their exposure to these highly carcinogenic chemicals. This was not the first time, nor would it be the last time our fighting men and women were treated like this.

During the World War II, another sixty thousand American soldiers were ordered to sign top secret statements never to discuss their "deliberate" exposure to mustard gas in "controlled tests." Some were injured so badly it took months for them to recover. Fifty years later, the Veterans Administration is seeking any survivors so as to understand the long-term effects that plagued them. Thousands more veterans were ordered to stand in the open during early atomic tests. Hundreds more unwittingly were administered LSD to study its effects. Agent Orange was rejected for two decades as a carcinogen, which sickened thousands exposed to it in Vietnam.

Anyone who has seen Steven Spielberg's movie *Saving Private Ryan* understands what was demanded of our veterans. Those injured by chemical warfare have been treated badly. For those who lost their legs, they were not made to crawl away from a discharge point in Iowa. The blind was not placed at the front gate of Fort Riley, Kansas, and ordered to find their way home; and those unable to move because of spinal damage were not dumped at the front gate of Fort McNair in Washington, DC, and arrested by the police for malingering. But this is how we treated our veterans who were poisoned with chemical warfare agents.

Since the dawn of history the empires of the Tigris Euphrates Valley have considered the area that today is Kuwait as its southern border. During the five hundred years of the Ottoman Empire, Kuwait belonged to Iraq. Millennia of Iraqi ownership came to an end with the arrival of the British after World War I. In mid-1958, Britain's colonial government in Iraq was overthrown by Colonel Abd al-Karim Qasim and two years later, he attempted to occupy Kuwait. British paratroopers in Kuwait convinced Baghdad to postpone its plans.

Following the third Arab-Israeli war in 1967, Iraq severed diplomatic relations with the United States and sought its future military requirements from the Soviet Union. Within five years, the Shah of Iran's armed forces possessed a huge fleet of American F-14 Tomcats, F-4 Phantoms, F-5 Tigers, air-to-air refueling tankers, hundreds of America's latest battle tanks and billions of dollars of associated hardware and munitions. Iraq was obviously concerned over long range Iranian and US intentions. Iran and Iraq have fought many wars since biblical times. Iran's population greatly outnumbered Iraq's while Iran's military forces were significantly stronger than Baghdad's. Another war seemed inevitable and Iraq began to consider chemical weapons as a mean to offset Iran's huge military advantage.

Iraq initially explored its chemical warfare requirements in Europe. They were warmly received there and found significant interest. Iraq's plans for huge new "chemical fertilizer factories" represented billions of dollars in new long-range contracts and Europe understood Iraq's intentions. The collapse of the Shah of Iran's government in 1978 and the chaos which followed quickly, convinced Baghdad that she could now defeat her worst enemy on the battlefield and eliminate the ex-Shah's formidable arsenal of American supplied weapons.

On September 15, 1980, Iraq attacked and destroyed a large part of Iran's army, navy, and air forces. But Iran's strategic depth prevented Iraq from conclusively defeating her on the battlefield and the war gradually became a stalemate. As the war progressed some 180 companies were heavily involved in helping Baghdad build the world's most modern chemical warfare facilities. Secretly involved were seventeen Austrian companies, eleven from Switzerland, seventeen French, eighty-six West German, twelve Italian, eighteen English, and twenty-nine from fourteen other countries. The only country missing was the United States. Everyone involved knew the international prohibitions against such weapons by the Geneva Convention and concealed their activities behind front companies. Provided within a few years was everything Iraq needed to manufacture over thirty-five thousand tons of the most advanced chemical, nerve and biological weapons!

The world watched in horror as hundreds of thousands of Iranians were systematically gassed and suffocated on the battlefield. Despite the huge losses, Iran's larger population seemed to point to her eventual victory. Fearful that Iran might break through Iraq's defenses and invade not only Iraq, but then Kuwait and Saudi Arabia as well, the United States secretly began transferring military technology to Baghdad. Washington resumed diplomatic relations with Baghdad in 1985. Many, at the time, wondered if Washington would condemn Iraq's use of chemical weapons. It didn't, and within a year, had joined the other countries secretly help building Iraq's chemical and biological warfare industries. Between early 1985 and August 1990, eighteen American companies joined the ranks of European companies already supplying not only chemical warfare factories but also the precursors needed to make chemical weapons. The American companies had household names like Allied Signal, Combustion Engineering and United States Steel. This frenetic buildup continued until the morning of August 2, 1990, when Iraq attacked Kuwait and made me a permanent guest of the state! Now Iraq was the "Great Satan" and Washington quickly moved to cover-up all traces of its part in supplying chemical weapons to Saddam Hussein.

In 1986 when the Iran-Iraq war ground to a halt and both sides signed a cease-fire, Iraq immediately turned its chemical warfare capability against its own people, the Kurds. Within a year 120,000 of them were dead; another eighty thousand were killed the following year. Many of those who did not die immediately from exposure were buried alive in a pit and covered up. Others became vegetables. Hikmut's brother-in-law, a newspaper editor in Erbil, showed me pictures of those that "survived." The killing continued until Iraq occupied Kuwait. Best known was the March 1988 gassing at Halabja, which received brief worldwide attention. Still Washington did not condemn Baghdad. By the end of 1988, Americans disgusted with Iraq reached such a fury that the senate unanimously passed the "Chemical and Biological Control Act" on January 25, 1989, ordering the President and the Executive Branch to stop exports of sensitive American chemical and biological warfare technology to Iraq.

A week later, the newly elected President, George Bush, vetoed the senate legislation and the flow of illegal help continued. Four months later, in May 1989, angered by continuing Pentagon exposure about its chemical and biological warfare exports to Iraq, the Bush administration ordered Dennis Kloske, of the Bureau of Export Administration at the Department of Commerce, to send a message to advise the Pentagon that the Department of Defense would no longer be involved in the review of American technology transfers to Iraq. Kloske said, "The development of biological and chemical weapons by Iraq, as well as the missile technology regime, are part of the foreign policy controls and are beyond the purview of the Department of Defense." Kloske's edict removed the last voice warning to the American people that dire consequences would follow.

By early 1990, Iraq had thirteen major chemical and biological warfare factories producing the most lethal weapons known to man. This production was being distributed to military depots and storage areas throughout southern and western Iraq. The weapons included aflatoxin, anthrax, botulinum toxin, mustard, lewisite, sarin, tabun, and VX. Iraq had produced almost seventy thousand tons of these weapons and had killed three hundred thousand Iranians and another four hundred thousand of its own Kurdish people in the northeastern mountains of Iraq. George Bush in Washington and his ambassador, April Glaspie in Baghdad, slept well despite the horrible set of events they had set in motion. Washington knew what was happening and they really didn't care.

In the early summer of 1990 a shipment of nuclear bomb detonators from California were stopped at Heathrow Airport in London and confiscated. Two days later Saddam Hussein made a public speech in Baghdad in which he concluded by saying, "We don't need an atomic bomb because our chemical weapons capability is only matched by the United States and the Soviet Union. May God's curse fall upon the big powers."

It didn't take long in coming. The United States was completely caught off guard on the morning of August 2, 1990. At 4:00 a.m. local time, six brigades of the Iraqi Republican Guard entered Kuwait and occupied the entire country!

For ten years prior to Iraq's occupation of Kuwait, intelligence agencies of the United States were watching Iraq's growing chemical warfare capabilities with mounting trepidation. Several other regional countries were also being watched, among them Syria and Libya.

By the time the Iran-Iraq war ended in 1988, intelligence files in Washington were bulging, and analysts were concerned because they knew the Iraqi leadership were unprincipled men who had already used chemical weapons against not only in Iran, but also their own people. Between 1987 and 1990 Iraq bought several new factories online, producing even more deadly biological and nerve toxins. Among these were anthrax, botulinum, and VX. The latter two were a million times more lethal than anything formerly available to Iraq. By the time of the Kuwait invasion, she'd produced another 36,250 tons of new chemical, nerve, and biological weapons and possessed enough VX to wipe out the entire population of Kuwait and Saudi Arabia! Available too, for the first time, were three hundred tons of anthrax and twenty-nine tons of botulinum toxins.

At the time of the invasion when President Bush drew his line in the sand, the Pentagon knew it could not protect American forces against Iraqi chemical weapons if Iraq used them. As more and more American fighting men arrived in Saudi Arabia and Iraq began deploying its chemical weapons into southern Iraq and Kuwait, American field commanders feared American casualties would approach 50 percent. The problem was finally resolved when Secretary of Defense Dick Cheney informed Saddam Hussein that his use of chemical or biological weapons against coalition troops would provoke a massive nuclear response from the West. Iraq had already deployed almost two-thirds of its available chemical, nerve and biological agents to Iraqi conventional munitions storage sites, most of which were within 150 miles of the Kuwait-Saudi border. It was not withdrawn and left in place.

In the days following the beginning of coalition air attacks on January 17, 1991, strikes inside Iraq included most known chemical production and storage facilities. Almost immediately, chemical detection equipment alarms across the Saudi Arabian border began ringing. Saddam Hussein's generals smiled. How stupid the Americans were! The prevailing southeasterly winds at that time of year were carrying away the airborne debris from the destroyed munitions storage areas towards the American lines in Saudi Arabia.

During the thirty-eight days after the coalition air campaign began on January 17, some seventy-five thousand combat missions were flown into Iraq. Among the targets attacked were scores of Iraqi conventional munitions sites at which chemical and biological weapons had been positioned. On thirty-one of the thirty-eight days, chemical detection alarms sounded among the coalition armies massed south of the Saudi and Kuwait border with Iraq, as the windborne plumes of chemical and biological debris drifted amongst them. The alarms were ignored.

By the time Operation Desert Storm got underway on the morning of February 24, 1991, American and coalition troops had already been repeatedly exposed to toxic clouds containing cocktails of chemical weapons drifting down on them from the damaged Iraqi chemical munitions dumps. Their cumulative exposure was about to become even more serious as the ground war began.

Official American military pre-invasion policy regarding the dangers of Iraqi chemical and biological weapons was based on four assumptions, all of which were false. If soldiers were not dying in masses on the battlefield then chemical or biological agents were not present, and if they had been, American troops had equipment to protect themselves from it. Furthermore, Iraq's chemical and nerve agent stockpiles were so unreliable and degraded that they posed little threat and the known stockpiles that did exist, when hit by coalition bombing, would be incinerated by blast and heat of the explosion.

The reality was quite different. First off, chemical exposure, like nuclear radiation, is a cumulative poisoning. Second, American protective equipment was totally inadequate. Third, Iraq's chemical weapons were as potent as or better than those in the US chemical warfare stockpiles and fourth, it was known that many chemical and biological weapons did not have flash points high enough to set them on fire in an explosion, thus their contents would be released into the atmosphere.

The Joint Chiefs of Staff, senior Pentagon leaders, and American field commanders in Saudi Arabia knew the true nature of the chemical and biological threat in the Gulf but chose to discount the threat. In the process, they needlessly endangered American troops. Department of Defense policy since the Gulf War is that no chemical or biological weapons were released by anyone. Therefore, American servicemen complaining of Gulf War Syndrome were imagining it, lying, or pretending to be sick.

In a 1996 interview, retired Army Major General Griffith, formerly the Commander of the 3rd Armored Corps which held the center of the US formations assaulting Iraq, testified he'd been extremely concerned about his post-war orders to send demolition teams to various chemical munitions dumps in southern Iraq and destroy them. Among them was the huge arsenal at Khamisiyah. Dozens of US demolition teams subsequently blew up these chemical dumps throughout southern Iraq in the days following the cease-fire. At several of these dumps, chemical detection alarms were sounded before and after the dumps were destroyed. General Griffith admitted his troops had found huge caches of intact and partially destroyed Iraqi chemical weapons, many of which were leaking from earlier coalition air attacks. General Griffith's testimony refutes his superior's written denials that no chemical releases took place.

Rolf Ekéus, the United Nations commander who took over from the United States after its troops left Iraq, visited Khamisiyah and was appalled at what his team found. Strewn everywhere throughout the dump were hundreds of damaged Iraqi chemical munitions, many of which were still leaking. He described the manner in which the dump was destroyed as naïve and unprofessional. When confronted with the UN findings the United States denied responsibility. Only the presence at Khamisiyah of hundreds of wooden crates bearing US production numbers for C-4 (an American military explosive) confirmed this. Only then did Washington finally recant its earlier denials.

Prevailing winds during the winter in Iraq are southeasterly as mentioned earlier and during a majority of the thirty-seven days of coalition air strikes and then again during the ensuing ground attack; plumes of chemical weapon toxins drifted across the 70 to 170 miles of desert into the massed coalition forces just across the Saudi-Kuwait border. None of these exposures in and of themselves were sufficient to kill, but cumulatively, the repeated exposures would bring more serious effects after the war. The effects of these exposures were detailed earlier in this chapter. Higher authorities repeatedly assured the troops that their sudden and recurring problems were unrelated to chemical weapons and were most likely resulted from a host of problems related to the desert environment in which they were living.

In the eighteen days after coalition armies moved into Kuwait and southern Iraq, sixteen more chemical detection alarms went off in Kuwait and an additional nine in Iraq. Many of the warnings in Kuwait were from multiple alarms including a spectrum of toxins ranging from mustard to lewisite, tabun, sarin, and soman. At several open-air munitions dumps in Kuwait, special American hazardous material teams (hazmat) suddenly appeared and took over responsibility for the removal of American-manufactured ordinance which contained Iraqi chemical weapons loads.

When the cease-fire came, a soldier from the 3rd Armored Division's 7th calvary was asked if it was worth it. "Gut level?" he replied, "Yeah! It was worth it. And for all those people back home that supported us, who believed in us, we do it for them." Thousands of these veterans who would soon wonder if their sacrifice really had been worth it. Many were sick even before they disembarked from aircraft flying them back home. But now the war was over and no one was interested in their problems. Those who sought medical attention were turned away and labeled complainers, malingerers, or trying to rip-off their government. Embarrassed, demeaned, and ashamed, most tried to deal with their illness outside the military, forcing many into poverty and bankruptcy as their health gradually worsened.

About 146 of the half million Americans involved in Desert Storm died on the battlefield. Experts declared the outcome a Pyrrhic victory. But in reality, the experience was one of the costliest four-day conflicts in American history. Within a year, so many veterans were swamping hospitals that Congress realized something was obviously amiss and authorized the National Institute of Mental Health to conduct a study on the long-term effects of exposure to mustard gas. The NIH report is of limited value insofar as it only addresses a single component of the cocktail of chemical, nerve, and biological agents, which the Gulf War veterans did or could, have encountered while involved in the Gulf War.

Once the victory parades ended across America and the troops went home, many of them began to realize they had serious medical problems. Among these were some, which are normally experienced by any army returning to a peacetime status, sleep disorders for instance. But there were other problems not formerly encountered among returning veterans for instance, mysterious skin rashes, muscle and joint pain, neuropsychological problems, shortness of breath, serious coughs and choking problems. Thousands of these veterans were advised their medical problems were of no consequence and they were sent away with prescriptions for aspirin and Excedrin!

As the flow of veterans flooding the hospitals and clinics increased, senior military leaders like General Colin Powell and General Norman Schwarzkopf repeatedly denied their exposure to chemical weapons during the Gulf War.

In April 1992, the Department of Defense issued a tome entitled, "Report to Congress, The Conduct of the Persian Gulf War." Page 639 points out that the thirty-eight-day air campaign against Iraq opened with "a sustained series of air attacks on all known chemical and biological sites." The 823-page report says nothing about chemical weapons problems during the war. Appendix Q, which dealt with chemical and biological warfare defense, spoke in glowing terms of the effectiveness of various defensive systems used, but makes no mention of any chemical alarms during the entire war!

As more and more veterans continued to besiege military and veterans' hospitals with Gulf War Syndrome, on May 25, 1994, General Shalikashvili, the new Chairman of the Joint Chiefs of Staff who replaced General Colin Powell, signed a letter emphatically stating there was no release of chemical, nerve, or biological weapons, accidentally or otherwise during the Gulf War. Shalikashvili lied and knew his statement was false. Major General Landry who was well known to General Shalikashvili and was formerly General Schwartzkopf's Chief of Staff in Saudi Arabia during the Gulf War, also stated at a hearing before Congress in which they were asking him why so many veterans had no stomach for modern warfare he said of the veterans, "Have you considered the possibility that a lot of these people are malingerers?"

Two things in retrospect are now clear: The United States provided considerable chemical and biological warfare technology to Iraq in the years preceding its occupation of Kuwait, and enabled that country to manufacture the most virulent nerve and biological weapons. Thousands of rounds of American manufactured munitions were found in Iraqi military storage dumps in both Kuwait and Iraq in the weeks after the war. Many of these munitions were loaded with Iraqi manufactured chemical and nerve agent loads. The Bush Administration however saw to it that special US hazmat teams (with Top Secret orders) showed up where ever these caches were found and immediately expedited their removal. Until today, it is unclear what became of this incriminating evidence of the Bush White House's participation in this issue. Senior Bush Administration staffers obviously knew that a firestorm would erupt if news of the President's insouciant secret activities ever became public knowledge. Thousands of US veterans who did President Bush's bidding had been exposed and were sick at his own hand.

You must be saying what can you do about it? First off, get mad, get *real* mad! These are our sons and daughters, our neighbors, loved ones, and our grandchildren who are being born with deformities; all in the name of democracy and freedom for all. Second, don't write to your congressman. He or she will tell you it really didn't happen, I'm a left wing, anti-government zealot, just plain nuts or they will take it under advisement. Pray to the God of your understanding? Perhaps, if you are a believer. There are many who should be brought to the bar of justice for their parts in this national calamity. But most important now is to recognize that hundreds of thousands of our veterans are sick because of their service to their country in the Gulf War. A national debate is needed to help them and how to prevent what happened to them from happening again!

EPILOGUE

You must be wondering, "What happened to all the people from all the places in this book?" Uncle Wally I never heard from again and in all likelihood is drunk somewhere in Canada. Dr. Tomasz, myself, my broker and a Saudi prince who bought Aristotle Onassis's apartment in New York City, tried to buy the Plaza Hotel but fell short. Doc was indicted by the Fed's in the infamous "Oil for Food" program to aid Iraqi relief but avoided charges by agreeing to identify high-ranking members of the Iraqi regime in the "Deck of 52" investigation and was aided by his new best friend, Sean Hannity. With the help of numerous letters from friends, family, and colleagues, he was exonerated of all charges primarily on the factor of his age. He went on to perform over four hundred blood transfusions on 9/11 right out on the sidewalk. He passed away from cancer several years ago. His former partner, Sam, was also indicted and didn't fare as well being given a lengthy-jail sentence but due to his military background he agreed to aid the U.S. with information about the Iraqi regime and beat all the charges.

Farqad is living a meager existence off his local accounting business and handouts from relatives in foreign countries. Naji got married and divorced and is living in California. Dr. Russell Smith took up a posting in Turkey and later succumbed to natural causes. Pat married a lovely Hungarian woman and settled in Northern Virginia. Colonel Bob retired from active duty and went into writing political novels. He also founded the Zor Foundation in Washington, DC of which I became a board member of. Zor was dedicated to fighting for human rights abuses as a result of the Gulf War and financial remuneration for hundreds of thousands of Kurds who suffered as a result of the fighting in addition to the gassing victims of Halabja which George Bush II later used as political fodder for his reelection to the presidency. Zor also spent eight years repeatedly pressing the US government to admit to causing Gulf War Syndrome and to seek the granting of medical benefits for not only the survivors but also the generations of their descendants to come. This was finally admitted to in a tiny article on the bottom of page eleven of the *New York Times*. The government of the United States did reluctantly accept culpability but not in so many words for causing the "disease." So much for "Weapons of Mass Destruction!"

John went through a quadruple bypass and survived but also went through yet another wife. Hikmut married his assistant, had three children, and with funding from me escaped to Turkey and then sought political asylum in Holland where he lives to this day and makes a living as an artist. His wife left him for a scurvy Egyptian but then came back to him. Oliver was going to build a hunting lodge but his wife passed, and he retired to Florida. Eli al-Haj was banished from Saudi Arabia over some alleged scandal. Saeed is still in the network business in Saudi Arabia. Saddam Hussein finally swung from a rope after more war and murder. His memory entrenched in the minds of millions. Tariq Aziz was kept alive and secreted away by the Americans as a useful asset even though he wanted to be executed as being a "true revolutionary" instead of a journalist turned politician. He passed away of natural causes. Joe Wilson III was sent by Washington on a wild goose chase to mid-Africa to look for evidence of "uranium cake" of which there was none. In the process, his wife was "outed" as a CIA asset, and they fell off the grid.

Lee went on to earn two law degrees. He befriended a human rights attorney in Washington DC who filed a class action suit for as many Iraq hostages as he could find against the Iraq government. It was known as the Hill case. Every hostage who was held until mid-December of 1990 was paid a handsome sum with frozen Iraqi assets here in the states of which the attorney took a 10 percent fee for each one of them. Lee and I were not part of this as this case it was over when Lee met him, and the State Department stopped the attorney from looking for any other hostages. But that did not deter him, and he found more and filed another suit known as the Vines case. However, George Bush II froze all Iraqi financial assets so with only US money to pay us (Lee and I now being part of it). It languished for the entire Bush presidency. When Obama and Hillary came to power, things picked up, but the settlement was nowhere near what the Hill decision was. It was based on a Senate formula of a flat award, plus money for everyday you were held captive. Since we escaped after five days, we did not fair very well, but the attorney still took 10 percent. Hillary Clinton reviewed specific cases and decided that if you met one of four criteria for physical abuse set by the Foreign Claims Settlement Commission while in captivity, you were entitled to another hearing before the panel of judges in Washington, DC.

I was the only one who had a real case having been dragged away at gunpoint. Lee did not, but he had recently seen the movie "Argo" about the Iran embassy hostages. In his mind, he concocted a scheme that he was pulled away from the group and put up against a wall in a "mock" execution. In an act of collusion between him and the lawyer for whom he did a lot of pro bono work, he was awarded one million dollars. When he returned to work in Washington, DC, he didn't have a scratch on him and told no one about his purported ordeal. Everyone in the office hated him to begin with. I told the truth and got nothing. I helped him get into law school, funded the numerous law contests he was a panel judge on, enabled him to get a job in the World Bank which "jump" started his career and this was the thanks I got. If you think there is such a thing as justice in this country, you are hallucinating. Even a letter from the wealthiest member of the Senate could not get them to reopen my case. A woman claimed she was raped by an Iraqi soldier in a Kuwait City hotel room after he followed her there from a bar. Although her claim stated she was examined by a physician at a nearby hospital she presented no physical evidence of injury nor any witness to the alleged act, just her word and her lawyer. She was awarded the sum of one million dollars in damages. Her occupation? Stripper!

I would like to express my apologies to peoples of all races, creed, or color for any remarks or descriptions that they may consider offensive. The opinions and conclusions I've drawn are from my own experiences and views and are not intended to cause malice nor injustice to anyone. I have steadfastly remained factual while trying to apply color to what was otherwise a terrifying and personal experience.

This book details my experience as an American private contractor working indirectly for the Revolutionary Command Council of Iraq for the year leading up to the invasion of Kuwait on August 2, 1990. What I witnessed firsthand, my incarceration as a hostage by their government, and my subsequent escape from the country. It reveals the truth about the massacres of the Kurds that took place in Halabja. The attempts to assassinate Saddam. The truth about the weapons of mass destruction including where they were, what they were, and how they were disposed of. The cover up by the US government of Gulf War syndrome and what it really was, why we refused to admit it, and the mistreatment of our veterans who suffered from it to this very day.

ABOUT THE AUTHOR

M r. John J. Norman is a management consultant having had a career that has spanned four decades, dating back to the early days of Information Technology in Silicon Valley to today's world of digital commerce. Mr. Norman is a graduate of New York Institute of Technology, where he majored in communication arts. He has worked in over forty countries and lived in many of them, thus experiencing an array of both professional and cultural challenges.

He has built, modernized and rehabilitated major financial institutions including private and commercial banks, state-owned banks, government ministries, and central banks around the world. Mr. Norman has spent over twenty-seven years on and off working in most countries in the Middle East as well as global "hotspots" such as Bosnia, Central Africa, Georgia, Yemen, and Pakistan. He was also CEO of a Dallas-based oil and gas exploration company as well as running, at the time, the largest online gaming company in the world.

CPSIA information can be obtained
at www.ICGtesting.com
Printed in the USA
BVHW07s1216221018
530870BV00004B/457/P

9 781643 503745